WHAT SHALL I DO WITH MY MONEY?

WHAT SHALL I DO WITH MY MONEY?

by Eliot Janeway

DAVID McKAY COMPANY, INC.   New York

For Elizabeth, Michael and William Janeway

Acknowledgments

THIS book was really proposed by my associate, Mrs. Betsy Flagler, and I was encouraged to embark on it by Miss Martha Kehoe and Miss Audrey Marks. Thanks go to them for their perspicacity in seeing the need for a book designed to help people protect their money in a time of economic insecurity, and for persuading me to write it in short order.

Special thanks also to my colleagues Sally Hardcastle, Salvatore Provenzale, Mrs. Molly Hartwig, Mrs. Gwenn Black, and Mrs. Barbara Wedgwood for their invaluable editorial and production help, and to Paul Reynolds, Marvin Strauss, and Arthur Laro for their advice and counsel on the manuscript. I am also indebted to Kennett Rawson, president of David McKay, for his cooperation in allowing me to interrupt work on a book to help or provoke the Government out of the difficulties it has brought down upon itself and upon all of us, in order to write this handbook on how to survive financially until the Government does find itself again.

I am grateful to my wife, Elizabeth Janeway, and to my

sons William and Michael for their helpful readings of the manuscript, and suggestions on how most intelligibly to bridge the gap that separates Americans who know how to read from those who know how to count.

Contents

	Introduction	1
I.	Diagnosis of the Trouble	11
II.	Managing Your Personal Finances	21
III.	Cash	43
IV.	Property	59
V.	Mutual Funds	87
VI.	Stocks—Principles	106
VII.	Stocks—Particulars	121
VIII.	Bonds	147
IX.	Advisors	174
X.	Omens and Portents	192
	Index	203

WHAT SHALL I DO
WITH MY MONEY?

Introduction

MOST of my analytical career has been spent in a commitment to optimism: to hopes, not to fears. Over the thirty-seven years that I've been putting my economic views and judgments before the public, I've been more often attacked for betting on growth and betterment than for glooming over threatening doom. If, recently, my judgment has shifted from warning that things were going to get better faster than expected, to alarms that they might grow worse at the same pace, these conclusions have been no more welcome to me than to my audience. But they are conclusions that can't be erased and could be costly to ignore. They have, consequently, prompted me to set forth a considered plan of action to deal with them.

The America in which I have grown up has enjoyed a pretty good run for its money. It is still enjoying a pretty good run even though it has run into trouble. The present situation may be dangerous, but it is retrievable; and, given the diagnosis as I have outlined it in the first and last chapters of this book, cures are not hard to find. There is no doubt, either, about who and who alone can dispense the cures—or more precisely, where and where alone victims must look for salvation. Only Government can undo the damage the Government has done. Washington is the only place where it can be done.

To add dimension to Lord Acton's famous warning about power, it institutionalizes not only corruption, but illusions as well. In the era that opened with FDR's assertion of Government's responsibility to act, a triple illusion grew up parallel to the power of modern Government in America: first, that it knows what it is doing; second, that it knows how to undo what it has done wrong; and third, that it has learned how to use its power to anticipate its problems instead of to retrieve its errors. Only recently have these comfortable assumptions come under suspicion, and even now Washington's ability to solve all problems without determined action on the part of individuals is still taken too much for granted.

Let's look at these happy-talk ideas again. First there's the strategic calculation of time, that is, of how long the present-day machinery of Government in America takes to respond to the pressure of problems it has permitted to get ahead of it, and to improvise the pragmatics of timely retrieval.

The clock is running out on the easy assumptions of universal affluence. A dividing line between beneficiaries of the inflationary crisis and victims is being drawn; and, more disturbing still, it is fluctuating. No prudent man, woman, family, business, or institution can be content to bet that the Government will retrieve the situation in time to spare them from getting caught on the wrong side of this shifting line. Until the Government learns how to know what it is doing and how to do what will work, it behooves the prudent to recognize that the Government does not know what it is doing and is not minded to find out what will work.

We are faced with an emergency that, until it is remedied by Government action, calls for the efforts of informed men and women to regain a hold over their own economic and financial situations. This is my reason for interrupting work on a book aimed at guiding the Government toward overall solutions to its problems in order to write this one, addressed to the Government's customers who vote its leaders in and out of office. While Washington wobbles, there's no more urgent priority than an effort to show people how to protect themselves and their money during the wait for Government to recognize both the problem and its solutions.

How long do they have to wait? Perspective on a prudent answer recalls the title of a memorable book by Judge (formerly SECC Chairman) Jerome Frank: *If Men Were Angels.* If they were, Frank explained, laws and courts of law would not be needed. If Governments were competent, everybody would be rich and relaxed, and yesterday's dynamic money managers in Wall Street would still be carefree geniuses. But men are not angels, and governments need guidance. Governments are always in a race against crises—increasingly so, with their active involvement in so many walks of life. The question about them is whether they will let themselves be helped before the onset of crisis hurts them.

Here is a short but specific list of necessarily partial

cures for the complaint with which the Government has affected itself and the securities markets and participants in them—as well as all the other conspicuously sick sections of economic society in America. I recognize that not one of these measures has the slightest chance of being considered, much less adopted, as matters stand in Washington today. They would be unpopular, and rightly so, for their immediate impact would be unpleasant, and in smaller, weaker economies some of them can hurt. But my judgment tells me that either they are in the cards— or something worse is.

Number one is credit controls. Number two is a Federal sales tax. Number three is a dividend tax credit combined with a tax credit for money spent on job training. Let me ask you to hold any negative reactions in abeyance while we see how they would work out in our present unprecedented situation.

The first of them, to be sure, has surfaced as a political token being passed back and forth between Congress and the Administration with an eye for record-making. The next, a Federal sales tax, has been held back from public view, but is already on wary professional display with each party to the political dispute waiting for the opportunity to blame necessity for imposing it upon the other.

But before going further into a discussion of my list, I must turn to the source of America's money troubles. This will be taken up more fully in later chapters. For the moment, it is enough to note that the source is the failure of the fiscal authorities to add up their obligations and, therefore, to calculate how much new money the Federal Government could raise by borrowing and how much beyond that it would need to raise by taxing. While the world of political finance is tangled in many complications, all of them nevertheless reduce themselves to one governing simplicity: every penny the Government spends that does not come from taxing comes from borrowing.

This simple fact makes clear that the country's money troubles are related to the Government's money needs and that these troubles are not economic. They are financial. It is the inflation of the cost of getting money which has all along been the primary cause of our overall inflationary distress, and which remains the cause today. And the inflation of money costs has been, and continues to be, a result of the fundamental failure of our Government to get its priorities straight—or, in old-fashioned language, to put the horse before the cart.

One of the reasons I stress this point is to warn against trusting any call to make mandatory wage and price controls a panacea. Under present circumstances, any attempt to freeze wages, while permitting interest rates and credit terms to tighten the screw on under-financed borrowers, would institutionalize inequity and invite chaos. Wage and price controls can be useful only in economic emergencies. In financial emergencies it is credit controls that are needed.

On June 18, 1970, I was invited to appear before the Joint Economic Committee's Subcommittee on Economy in Government to outline my answers to the present problems, and I stressed then, as I stress now, that they cannot be regarded as a panacea, either. On the contrary, the remedial program I put forward then represents the emergency financial expedient needed to ward off a recurrence of the kind of panic that America resolved, a full generation ago, never to suffer again.

As I have said, the first of these emergency measures is credit controls. Our country today finds itself afflicted with a new disease called "all-at-once-itis," which has been spread by the competition between Government and business for money. It is not, however, this borrowing itself which is inflationary, but rather excessive borrowing in relation to what prove to be insufficient earnings. In the case of the Treasury, these under-earnings are short-falls in tax receipts. The main thrust of credit controls would be to substitute permanent capital for borrowings. It would invite business to go to the stock market for the money it needs, and thus call off the competition between business and Government borrowers. Overnight, this would engineer a dramatic and sustainable downward movement in long-term interest rates as business surrendered the long-term credit market to that greediest of money-users, the Government.

Now, it's certainly true that the stock market would have been much better able to bear the burden of refinancing debt into equity when it was high and strong than now, when it is low and weak—indeed, one of the desirable economic functions performed by a buoyant stock market is to effect such refinancing. But the damage has been done, and the load of debt waiting to be refinanced or repudiated is dangerous. The future open to the stock market today doesn't include a surge to new highs but merely the choice between a rout and a relatively orderly retreat.

But whether it is a rout, or merely a retreat, bottom

will not be hit until long-term interest rates have been brought down low enough to make a safe landing for the market possible. Credit demands being what they are, from bigger businesses and all levels of governments in America, long-term interest rates will not come down until Washington brings them down.

But essential though credit controls are to lower long-term interest rates, by themselves they will not be enough to do the job. Even with the entire long-term credit market at their disposal, state and local as well as Federal Governments will still find themselves short of the money they need to finance their commitments. Hence the unhappy but indecisive mutters being heard about the need for a Federal tax increase.

Now an admission by the proprietors of political power that a Federal tax increase is needed invites them to present themselves to the business end of a political buzz saw. The reason is that familiar and relatively acceptable methods of raising revenues are out, including a stepped-up income tax. Both houses of Congress were in bipartisan agreement that no more revenue could be raised by going the income tax route even before the profit squeeze on business and the collapse of the stock market shut it off as a credible approach.

Just as Government can raise money in only one of two ways—by taxing or by borrowing—so it can raise tax revenue in only one of two ways, by taxing incomes or transactions. The name for a tax on transactions is a sales tax, and sales tax is a bad word. Nevertheless, because governments and businesses are all busted, while the retail public has money and is spending it, painful realism makes clear that the only place the Treasury can hope to look for the solution to its problem is where the big buck is changing hands and is readily available—at the retail cash register.

On the merits, a sales tax would be a bargain for the public if it worked. And it would work. Because in a country spending $600 billion at retail, suffering more than a six percent rate of inflation, a three percent sales tax raising $18 billion would avoid $18 billion of the Federal borrowings which are pushing up interest rates and powering the inflation.

I repeat, I do not see this measure as being politically feasible at this time, no matter how effective it might be financially. The same holds true for my next medicinal dose, as I recognized when I presented it to the Joint Economic Committee, to be combined in a package with credit controls. This is the enactment of a dividend tax credit. Such legislative action would mean an abrupt about-face by the Administration on its decision to rescind the investment tax credit, and a reversal like this is never welcomed by the "Ins." Nonetheless, a dividend tax credit would be a much more efficient and economic stabilizer than the present desperate recourse to emergency spending and lending.

The reason is that a dividend tax credit would ease the burden of servicing dividends on corporations as they increase their supply of equity capital. The way it would work would be to allow corporations to service their dividends, as they do interest on their debt, before taxes, instead of after. Any hope of remobilizing the stock market to absorb the enormous burden of capital corporations must raise to pay off their load of unsecured and insupportable debt rests upon their ability to pay investors going rates of dividends.

In recognizing that it might not be politically acceptable at the moment—looking, as it does on the surface, like a gift to the rich—I suggested to the Economic Committee that it could be packaged more acceptably if it was combined with a job training tax credit that would encourage employers to undertake to provide vocational skills for those at present unemployable because underprivileged.

Even so, the Chairman of the Subcommittee, Senator William Proxmire, was skeptical about the chances of this measure being considered by Congress this year or next.

My reply to him then, and it covers the remedies I am putting to my readers here, was: "What may seem politically unacceptable or unthinkable with the telephone company's stock yielding six percent, Congress may be very grateful to have an opportunity to vote for with telephone company stock yielding 10 percent; which I would equate with the Dow-Jones average at 250, with corporation after corporation saying, How can we afford to pay dividends with our creditor's money?" I do not mean to be taken as predicting that the Dow-Jones average will be driven anywhere as low as 250—clearly a disaster level. But I do mean to be taken as warning that no magic number represents bottom for the stock market; and that it will not hit bottom until the financial crisis in Washington has been brought under sufficient control to signal a significant and sustainable drop in long-term interest rates.

Fear is a great compromiser. These proposals are workable, and as time runs out, they will become increasingly acceptable and even welcome. The more drastic the deterioration in conditions, the faster the rate at which the workable becomes acceptable as the feasible.

CHAPTER I

Diagnosis of the Trouble

THE arrival of the 1970s has injected a big new question into the investment debate: how are we to adjust from the last decade of affluence to the new decade of strain upon affluence?

All during the postwar boom, inflation ran neck and neck with affluence. This meant that, while money was worth a little less, everybody had a lot more of it. But the arrival of 1970 switched the deal. Now, suddenly, everyone's money is worth a lot less, and everyone is scared of running out of money—the richer they are, the greater the fear—and with good reason.

The obvious financial question about today's picture is whether the new decade will measure continued gains by money-users or whether it will score the first setback for them since the 1930s. There is also a third alternative, which would add up to a lesser evil for the country, but cause a lot of trouble for its money-users. This is that the country will spin its wheels, going nowhere, while its money-users run out of gas. No need to do any double-domed theorizing about this danger. It is what has been happening in the economy and what has been going wrong in the stock market.

The present generation of money-users grew up confident of staying ahead of the game without trying or worrying. For over a year now, everyone has been on notice to run scared—of quite *what*, most of them are not too clear. The question is whether it is safe to relax and play for time before the old game starts up again or whether to head for the sidelines and not to run at all.

As with the big picture, there is a third alternative for money-users who want to know what to do with their money while inflation dominates the big picture and deflation breaks the stock market. It is that an altogether new money game may be starting up. This is what I think. The way to figure out how to play it is to find out what went wrong with the old game.

It is axiomatic that no two market disturbances ever occur in exactly the same way. The importance of historical analysis, over and above all that knowledge is worth for its own sake and what historical perspective is worth as a guide to balanced judgment, derives from the light it sheds on the difference between each new boom and the last, and between each new bust and the last. Again and again, the biggest changes in business and financial history come as the biggest surprises.

The present crisis of inflation in the country and of deflation in the stock market has come as the biggest surprise yet. But a quick flashback will explain how the early financial history of America is repeating itself.

Since America came of age, after World War I, her dollar troubles have been largely due to failures of economic demand—not enough buyers for wheat or cars or plane seats, etc. But while she was growing up, her troubles were due to running out of money. In 1970, America has taken a long step back to that year of money trouble, 1907.

The Liquidity Panic of 1907

One good reason why the liquidity panic of 1907 is relevant today is that the shock of its impact set in motion the legislative wheels which created the Federal Reserve Board with a mandate to prevent the recurrence of a money shortage. Before then, it was only the disease itself that killed. This time around, the old-fashioned doctor, the Federal Reserve Board, has been aggravating the trouble. The connection between what went wrong for the country in 1907 and what went wrong in the stock market was no chicken-and-egg proposition. Then, as now, the stock market ran out of buyers when the financial system ran out of money.

The late, great Paul M. Warburg, the father of the Federal Reserve system, wrote the epitaph on the fiasco of 1907 when he said, "Rates of 50 to 100 percent could not bring money, because our system—or rather our lack of system—had killed our confidence in our own credit."

The disaster of 1907 interrupted the heartbeat of the economy at a time when the country was waiting to enjoy unprecedented industrial expansion, to spread unimagined financial benefits, and to produce unexpected social improvements—all this in a simple domestic setting uncomplicated by military and social burdens, or by taxes, and financed by generous and continuous arrivals of money and manpower from abroad.

By 1908 the economy was up and on its way again. The

pragmatic test of prosperity recovered was furnished at the polls. Although the Republicans were the "Ins" in 1907, and had refused to move on monetary reform, the economic recovery was swift and sharp enough to renew their political mandate in the 1908 Presidential election. The fact that they won with a bumbling old stooge like Taft means that they could have won with anybody!

The flashback to the panic of 1907 is relevant because it recalls how the market was broken when the system ran out of money. A parallel flashback to 1929 is relevant, too, for three good reasons. The first is political: by 1929, America had come of age internationally and was burdened by international investments (mainly hinging on her efforts to collect uncollectable war debts). The second is psychological: 1929 is the year on everybody's mind —because of both the hope that it could never happen again and the fear that it may. I hasten to say that, paradoxically, both the hope and the fear are realistic; which brings up the third reason why 1929 is relevant in 1970— as a study in contrast for the future. The 1929 collapse in the stock market started a chain reaction which ended by collapsing the entire world economy; the sequence was crash-and-depression. But, although the tragic history of 1929 has been repeating itself in the stock market, it will not happen again outside Wall Street.

The trouble that started in 1929 took a long time to unwind. In fact, in the end it was unwound the hard way. Neither the recuperative power of the economy nor the wisdom of its leadership spared it the ordeal of a wholesale liquidation of debts and deflation of assets. Such debacles had been suffered by modern Germany and by modern France, but in both cases as the result of runaway inflation. America's financial collapse from 1929 to 1933 was the first comparable tragedy to have been generated by runaway deflation

The deflation of the Old Deal climaxed in the failure which set the stage for the political success of the New Deal. The New Deal rewrote the rules of the money game, but it took war to start enough money moving fast enough to get the economy moving at full speed again. World War II especially benefited those people who learned how to play by the new rules that the New Deal had written. The money game that was good through the great war and postwar boom of the 1940s, 1950s, and 1960s is the game that ended with the arrival of the 1970s.

The Crash of 1929 and the Breathing Spell of 1930

In the folklore of the history of panics, the year 1929 (when the Federal Reserve Board was already 16 years old and old enough to know better!) stands out as the distinctive, apocalyptic year. But 1929 was not the year of Humpty-Dumpty; it was merely the year in which the wall on which Humpty-Dumpty was sitting developed its first big telltale crack.

The fall that was to prove fatal did not come until later. To be precise, it did not come until 1931. The fateful year of entrapment, which turned the setback of 1929 into the calamity of 1931, was the year of false recovery in 1930; 1930 belongs alongside 1907 as a year to ponder for the 1970s.

The speculative rally of 1930 was almost universally assumed at the time to have blown away the ill winds which knocked the stock market over in 1929. In fact, it did more damage than the initial break which folklore has dramatized and which history has institutionalized.

Any number of realists, who had been prudent enough to run scared before the market took its beating in 1929, were suckered back into the presumed recovery rally in 1930. They assumed that what had been knocked down had been made cheap simply because it had been knocked down. The great bear market rally of 1930 painted over the crack in the wall on which Humpty-Dumpty was sitting and set him up for his great fall.

These two flashbacks—to the panic of 1907 and to the crash-and-depression which followed 1929—illustrate the difference between *panic* and *depression*, which are the two words most often used to describe the worst kinds of pocketbook trouble.

Panic hits when money-users, beginning with the Government, which is the biggest money-user of all, run out of cash and cannot get credit. Depression develops when a crash that begins in the stock market ends by shutting down the economy. Another 1907 is a clear and present danger for now. Another 1929 is not.

The contrast with each year of trouble is as helpful as the comparison between each of these years of big trouble.

The trouble of 1907 was painful but short and brought no political complications. The trouble of 1929 built up into a long, agonizing sequence of financial, economic, political, social, and military convulsions, both inside America and internationally. For the big picture today— that is, for the mass of American families as distinct from Wall Street's "New Poor"—the danger of another 1929 is more political and social than financial or economic.

Recession, Depression, Panic—or Readjustment?

If panic is the danger for money-users that has been ignored, and depression is the danger for the big picture that has been dramatized, recession is the popular false alarm for the economy.

The difference between recession and depression is simply stated: it is the difference between a business slowdown and a financial breakdown. When a recession hits people make a little less money. A depression gets out of hand when people lose not only their incomes but their businesses, their homes, their savings, and even their sources of subsistence. This is not going to happen today or tomorrow.

Another difference between a recession and a depression is that a recession brings a corrective breather to the economy and its markets, while a depression knocks it out of commission.

A panic interrupts the workings of the markets. A stock market panic can coexist with an economic expansion. In fact, it did in 1917 when the stock market was shut down amid a record war boom. This seemingly paradoxical history of Wall Street panic and Main Street prosperity could repeat itself today.

Contrary to popular fears, the bad news a recession brings for the big picture is not necessarily bad news for the stock market. The great illusion is that stock prices go up when business activity speeds up and vice versa. The reality to remember is that a favorable stock market trend depends less upon favorable business conditions than upon favorable money conditions. A recession—the technical term for business slowdown—brings better money conditions and tilts the stock market upward. By the same token, better business means bigger money demands. This signals good news for the economy and adds up to bad news for the stock market.

So much for theory—the fact is that the theoretical argument about recession, like the memory of depression, has distracted attention from the practical danger of panic.

How Inflation Has Climaxed
by Deflating the Stock Market

The most popular cliché about inflation is that the prices of stocks go up as fast as the cost of living and of doing business, and, therefore, that the place to beat it is in the stock market. But this simple supposition about inflation has just turned out not to be true. So has the simplistic supposition that the way to slow inflation down is to slow down the economy into a recession. But the biggest surprise of all is coming with the realization that an inflation, which is drenching the economic landscape with torrents of money, can climax in a panic that has been drying up the markets for lack of money.

Financial functions parallel physiological ones. Breathing, for example, is a function common to all living things —human, animal, plant, and marine. Borrowing faster than earning is the function common to all inflations.

Today businesses are borrowing faster than they are collecting, State and local governments are borrowing even faster than they are raising tax rates—and that's going some!

Historically, in the days before big governments and little wars, there was a rhythm between borrowers and borrowing. When business borrowed, government didn't;

when government borrowed, business didn't—as simple as breathing out and breathing in. Moreover, when the Federal Government was a big borrower, state and local governments didn't borrow.

Today, every government in the country—from the U.S. Treasury to South Knee Cap, North Dakota—*and* business are in competition for all the dollars they can borrow, spreading a new disease called "all-at-once-itis"—and it's a real killer.

Governments always stick with the old remedy book after new conditions have suspended some of the old rules and reversed others. They never anticipate their problems, or insure the money-users (on whom they depend for taxes) against their failure to solve them. But investors invariably speculate on new government policies insuring stability just when old government commitments compound risks.

The American Government has stuck with the old rule that the way to slow down inflation is to make money more expensive and harder to get. The new reality is that this speeds up inflation. The result of this miscalculation has been another surprise: this is the first inflation in history to have put a premium on cash.

The government has overstayed with another outworn rule in playing its so-called "game-plan" against inflation as a game against the stock market. Because past inflations have run neck and neck with inflations in stock prices, the Government strategists have assumed that the place to begin beating back the present inflation was in the stock market. They have wrecked the stock market, but inflation has wrecked their policies.

While inflation is real enough as a measure of increases

in the cost of living and doing business, it is a misleading and tricky abstraction as an investment guide. A new double standard has developed for gauging the risk-reward ratio as it applies to the economy and as it applies to investors. The economy is underwritten by the fact that Government knows enough to minimize the risks of depression even if it does not know enough to capitalize on the rewards of stability. But the Government's underwriting of the economy does not extend to its investment markets. On the contrary, the way in which the Government is financing the insurance it is providing against depression is at the expense of its investment markets. For the first time since 1929, investors are confronted by more investment risks than opportunities.

What investors and Government policy-makers alike need is a new financial first-aid book.

Here it is. It's an opportunity for the investment community's silent majority to steal a march on the articulate elite of market sophisticates who pride themselves on making and breaking investment fashions.

CHAPTER II

Managing Your Personal Finances

MR. MICAWBER, the character in Charles Dickens's *David Copperfield*, who was always inventing muddle-headed schemes for making great fortunes and counting on good luck tomorrow to bail him out of his continuing insolvency, summed up his mishaps with the sad observation: "Annual income twenty pounds, annual expenditure nineteen shillings and sixpence, result happiness. Annual income twenty pounds, annual expenditure twenty pounds ought and six, result misery."

Happiness may involve more than that extra jolly sixpence, but more outgo than income does indeed add up to misery. In a simpler day, when everyone was clear about the necessities of life, there was little trouble in agreeing where to draw the line past which to hold off on spending and to start saving. The family budget was made to mean just what the words said—for those who had the money as well as for those who were trying to get it. But today the old lines between necessities and luxuries are blurred. So is the old distinction between cost of living and standard of living.

Just as, in the age of simple technology, education meant the "three R's," so not too many decades ago, "cost of living" still referred to the traditional subsistence cost of food, rent, and clothing, plus not very much more in the way of extras for transportation, and sickness, and a few frills, like education or an occasional holiday paid for by savings. But in today's topsy-turvy world, yesterday's luxuries have mushroomed into necessities. (Before the automobile polluted the air, it was a luxury. Now that it has polluted the air, air-conditioning is becoming a necessity even in cool weather.)

While the claims on spending have left less and less room for savings, the incentives for speculation have made savings seem less of a necessity. The general complaint that the Government has lost all sense of priorities is duplicated in the example of families at a loss to fix their own priorities—starting with the expenditures that are inescapable and aiming at ways and means of putting money to work to buy personal security and to invest in increasing their personal prosperity.

The costs of food, shelter, and clothing still claim top priority on current income, but they are no longer the only current expenses that do. It's nothing new to say that health costs are a big factor, too. They always were, in times of medical emergencies. But now that yesterday's quick killers have been turned into today's costly cures, whopping medical and dental bills occur all year round.

The servicing of appliances and automobiles accounts for another new priority on irreducible living costs. The cost of inflation has been loaded not only onto the cost of buying equipment, but also onto the cost of servicing it—understandably so, because the servicing of equipment is mainly labor. In many parts of the United States, the cost of keeping a car is part of the cost of keeping a job. And the cost of buying appliances is part of the cost of the wife-mother leaving home to take a job and of the husband-father taking on a second job. Everyone caught with the basic necessity of investing in hard goods has no choice but to pay to keep them in good and constant repair.

Back when subsistence meant little beyond food, clothing, and shelter, the simple rule of thumb was that it was not prudent to spend more than 25 percent on rent. That rule still holds—when it is possible to hold to it! Today rents are rising nearly as fast as medical costs. Both are running away nearly as fast as property taxes, which, on reflection, add up to surcharges on rent. No matter whether families own their own homes or have leases, any budgeting for cost of rent wants to be adjusted upward for the big runaway increase in the cost of government— namely, property taxes.

The inflating cost of rent is the "big swing" factor in family budgeting. Food, clothing, travel, and luxuries are the more readily controllable constants. Any family with rent costs over 25 percent of its net take-home pay, after taxes and interest charges, is likely to do no better than run on a log if everything goes well; and it is certain to fall off that log the minute something goes wrong.

Given 25 percent of net usable income for rent as the first rule for family budgeting, the 10 percent put-away rule is the second. A cash savings account equal to six months pre-tax income is a bare minimum for anyone minded to graduate into investment status. Families with health problems will obviously need more.

Add insurance to the growing list of necessities that are fixed charges on income. Families prudent enough to meet the first priority of budgeting and, in addition, to build a cash reserve are likely to be prudent enough to buy insurance while the insured are still young and healthy enough to get it cheaply. The families prudent enough to meet these priorities are also likely to accumulate investment assets. The more they do, the less dependent they will be upon insurance to buy them all the protection they will need. But until they do build investment assets, they will need more, rather than less, insurance.

Insurance is the biggest bargain anyone can buy today, and the earlier the age at which it is bought, the bigger the bargain. Not that the insurance companies are giving anything away, and not that they aren't having their own troubles along with everyone else. But they are on the profitable side of one great change which enables them to establish the cost of protection against the financial impact of death as the one bargain ingredient in prudent family budgeting while the cost of everything else has gone up. The profitable gimmick responsible for the bargain life insurance companies sell is measured by the dramatic lengthening of life expectancy. Premiums are still set according to the old mortality tables, which assumed shorter life expectancy. The longer the life insurance companies can collect premiums and delay the day of reckoning announced by the death of the policyholder, the longer they can enjoy more premium income. The cheap cost of straight life insurance policies remains the one outstanding inflation-proof bargain in today's inflationary jungle.

The purpose of insurance is protection. It is a bargain

only so long as protection is what is bought. The insurance salesman will talk of it in terms of both protection and investment, but when, in a 10 percent money market, insurance only gets you a 4 or 5 percent return, you pay a high price if you believe him.

Life insurance is simply a method of providing money for someone when you die. In return for the payment of premiums, a life insurance company guarantees that, from the moment it writes your policy, it will pay the full face amount of the policy upon your death.

In order to understand why life insurance is such an important financial tool and why it is needed by so many people, consider what a person would be faced with if life insurance was not available. Take the situation of a young man with a wife and two children who has a good job and is able to save some money. He would like to enjoy some of the luxuries of life, but is concerned about how his family would survive financially if he were to die before he could save enough money to provide for them. Without the opportunity to buy life insurance, he finds that he must defer his enjoyment of the things he wants until he can build the kind of nest egg his family would need. This could take ten, twenty, or more years. Life insurance provides it instantly.

Life insurance companies provide three main kinds of assets: term and permanent life insurance, and annuities. Term insurance provides nothing but death protection. It is issued for a period of time and is not automatically renewable beyond this period. When the policy expires, the policyholder receives nothing. It is best suited for a short-term need such as when insurance is required in connection with a loan or a plane trip.

The premium which the insurance company charges for term insurance is based upon the current age of the insured and increases as the insured gets older. In a typical term policy the premium would increase every five years.

Term insurance may be renewable or non-renewable, and it may be convertible or non-convertible.

For example, a five-year *non-renewable* term policy would continue for a period of five years, after which the policy could not be continued. A five-year *renewable* term, on the other hand, could be renewed every five years, regardless of the policyholder's health, with an increase in premium each time a new five-year period begins. Even a renewable term policy cannot be renewed indefinitely. Typically, the cutoff age is sixty-five or seventy.

A convertible term policy is one that gives the policyholder an option to convert his policy to permanent insurance regardless of his health.

Permanent insurance is the second basic type of life insurance and, as the name implies, is designed to provide for needs that are long-term in nature. Examples of such needs are: the need for capital from which the family can derive an income if the father dies; the need to provide money for estate taxes and administrative costs; the need to provide the family with a cash reserve or emergency fund; and the need to provide smaller businesses with working capital if their proprietors die at awkward times.

Since permanent insurance is expected to remain in force for a long period of time, the insurance company is able to charge a level premium for the insured's lifetime. This premium depends upon the age at which the insurance is taken out, but unlike term insurance, the premium for the policy does not increase as the policy gets older.

Also unlike term, permanent insurance may be continued for as long as the insured lives.

Some extreme critics of insurance allege that policyholders can pay as much in premiums as is eventually paid out in death benefits. But this is possible in only exceptional cases—for example, when a man takes out a policy late in life, is paying a high premium, and lives on into very old age. The argument also ignores the fact that throughout the time the policy is in force its holder has received protection and the beneficiaries receive the full face amount whether he has paid one or a dozen premiums. In every state, insurance is rigorously supervised and regulated, and complaints against policies generally arise only because holders have chosen the wrong kind to suit their needs. As with everything else you buy, you get the insurance you pay for.

Permanent insurance, in addition to providing a death benefit, provides an element of savings called cash value, which the insured receives if he cancels his policy, or against which he has the right to borrow at a fixed interest rate with no obligation to repay. Contrary to the standard criticism of life insurance that inflation wipes it out, this feature of cheap, "no questions asked" borrowing power offers a can't-lose, built-in protection against inflation. No protection is more safe or profitable against the usurious interest rates and credit squeezes in which inflation climaxes than the borrowing power that builds up in permanent life policies. And any loan on a policy can be covered by special term insurance.

The three most common types of permanent insurance are whole life (also called straight or ordinary life), limited-payment life, and endowment. All have the elements of permanent insurance just discussed.

Whole life has the lowest premium of the three and calls for a level premium for as long as the insured lives, i.e., his whole life. Of course, the policyholder may cash his policy in at any time if he wants to.

Limited-payment life has a higher premium but becomes fully paid up at the end of the specified period. Twenty-payment life, for example, becomes fully paid up at the end of twenty years. After twenty years, the policy remains in effect without any additional premium payments, and the full face amount of the policy is paid to the beneficiary when the insured dies.

Endowment, in addition to providing death protection, provides that the full face amount of the policy will be paid at the end of the endowment period, typically twenty years, to the living insured. Very few endowment policies are bought today because of the extremely high premium that has to be paid for the amount of insurance protection obtained.

An annuity provides an income for as long as the policyholder lives. This is the reverse of life insurance. Life insurance provides financial protection after death.

The most common type of annuity is the single-premium immediate annuity. Under this arrangement, the policyholder makes a single payment to the insurance company, in return for which he receives a monthly income from the company for as long as he lives. The older the policyholder is when he buys the annuity, the more his monthly income will be. This is true because the insurance company expects to have to make fewer payments to an older person.

A second type of annuity known as the annual-premium deferred annuity provides the same benefits, but spreads premium payments over the years prior to retirement, instead of requiring the payment of premium in one lump sum.

Generally, annuities are best suited for and provide the greatest benefit to older people interested in a high income with no desire to pass capital on to someone else.

The question of how much life insurance to buy wants to be considered by several standards. (1) The earning power of the principal earner in the family; (2) educational obligations to children; and (3) the earning power and health of the rest of the family. In this day of increasing participation for wives, mothers, and grandmothers in productive employment, it is economic for husbands and wives to insure each other's lives.

Debt is another consideration in setting guidelines for how much insurance protection to buy. Inflation creates incentives to owe, but debt creates exposure to the loss of earning power when interest and amortization payments are still falling due.

The prudent way for the future investor to begin buying insurance is to buy the equivalent of five years' worth of pre-taxed earned income plus at least the first five years' worth of any mortgage and/or short-term debt. This may hurt at the start, but it will help long before the finish. Once insurance has covered the family's line of retreat, the coast is clear to start accumulating for investment. Meanwhile, insurance provides the economic way to assure enough cash to family survivors to keep the sheriff away. This way a borrower buys protection and insures that his estate will be liquid on his death.

Investment ranks a poor third for the prudent in the order of money-using priorities—after cash reserve, and insurance. It is an unpleasant, but unavoidable financial fact of life that people with just a few thousand dollars on hand are still in the savings class; and far from having graduated into the investors class.

But the chances are that any family wise enough to budget for emergencies, for insurance, and for investment will participate in the general increase in earned incomes. As it does, it can begin to rely on its investment (supplementing its insurance) to stay within reach of the goal of maintaining capital equal to five years of pre-tax income plus five years' worth of debt.

Families tending to overspend tend not to save at all. By the same token, families tending to save tend to over-save, making too much of the first good rule of family budgeting into a bad rule by under-investing. Again and again, families saving themselves into sanctuaries against the rising cost of living have over-saved and under-invested. But the prudent families saving themselves into an investment stance are not likely to stop saving because they continue investing.

Q. What do you think is the most workable form for setting up a family budget?

Mr. W. D. (Tulsa, Oklahoma)

A. Begin by calculating your family health costs for the last five years, separating the unpredictable, recurring sickbills everyone has from the predictable nonrecurring ones (such as childbirth). Then calculate the number of times you have moved in the last five years, getting clear the condition of your neighborhood, your home, and your family plans as to whether you may expect to move in the next five years. In this perspective, see how close you come to keeping your home costs—including property tax, maintenance, and repairs—down to 25 percent of combined family income. Be sure to balance your expectations for higher earning against education expenses you can anticipate. An increasing number of families are learning to break even on living expenses and family obligations on what the head of the household earns, relying on the wife's going to work to build up savings reserves and to earn the makings of an investment program.

Q. I find I'm over my head with installment purchases. Is there some sort of guideline about how much of my current income should be used to pay off debts on on-time purchases?

Mr. L. N. (Andover, Massachusetts)

A. The place to begin is to stop buying. You would do better switching your shopping time to moonlighting or overtime, if you can get it. From the sound of your question, no rule of thumb is likely to do you very much good. For someone in your squeeze, any ratio is too high.

Q. How can I budget my family's income soundly when rent increases keep going through the roof?

Mr. W. H. (Stratford, Connecticut)

A. This problem exists even in cities, such as New York, which are supposedly protected by rent controls. In that number-one concentration of apartment-house living, rents are admittedly rising faster than anywhere else in the country—if only because property taxes and labor costs are rising; and landlords are passing the increases on to their tenants. The worst inflator of all is the rent-controlling city government itself: as fast as landlords go broke and drop substandard properties for back taxes, the city takes over and jumps rents, on the blunt proposition that its rent-control rules apply to landlords but not to itself. As far as your budget goes—and it is less than likely to go far enough—try to err on the side of prudence. The rent explosion is one very good reason for building an emergency cash reserve as a top priority. Moving to lower-grade housing may seem to be an obvious economy, but it will not protect you. One of the characteristics of the present rate of runaway is that the lower-grade the dwelling, the steeper the rate of inflation. Only upper-group accommodation—traditionally sensitive to the stock market—is coming down in price.

Q. How much should I plan to save out of my income?

Mr. J. E. (Detroit, Michigan)

A. John D. Rockefeller the first didn't become the richest man in the country by saving every dime on the dollar. Doing so is no passport to wealth, but it is a way of building up cash past the great divide between savings (held in reserve against emergencies) and investment availability.

Two simple rules of thumb explain why it is important to save enough to build first a cash-reserve emergency fund and then to keep building it up for investment. The first is that during the last two war emergencies—World War II and the Korean War—the Government took a 20 percent bite for compulsory savings (for which it paid with the legalized swindle known as E-bonds—see Chapter VIII on bonds). The second is that the prudent family is on double notice nowadays that: (1) any of the three governments, city, state, or Federal, to which it is subjected, may take an extra 10 percent tax bite out of its usable income at any time; and (2) that even if one of the governments doesn't, or even because it doesn't (the inflation in the cost of government being the alternative to inflation in the cost of living), inflation is now eroding a budgetable 10 percent of everybody's income a year.

Anyone saving 10 percent of pre-tax income a year is getting one jump ahead of either the tax collector or inflation, as well as having the use of the money. With this rate of saving, you are therefore buying the right to put your money to work, and earning a return on investment as a continuous payback against the rising cost of governments and against the rising costs of inflation.

Q. For several years I have been following your columns in the Chicago Tribune, so I know you think that rules aren't too reliable these days. But, more and more, you have been mentioning cash reserve and savings before investing. I have always believed that a cash reserve should amount to two months' salary. A friend of mine now tells me that in this day and age it ought to be six months' salary. Would you be willing to generalize as to ratios of cash reserve, savings, and investing to monthly or annual salary?

Mr. W. S. (Evanston, Illinois)

A. Six months equivalent of pre-tax income is a minimum cash reserve. Any family with health problems probably needs more. The 10 percent set-aside rule is a minimum for cash beyond this. But, once you have gone conservative in setting aside cash reserve and observing the 10 percent savings rule, don't rush to the other extreme by oversaving beyond 10 percent. Invest anything and everything you can as fast as you can get 10 percent ahead of the rat race.

Q. Does it make sense to set aside any money for speculating? Or should I try to save all the income I don't spend?

Mr. T. P. (Cleveland, Ohio)

A. The prudent and profitable distinction between savings and investment suggests another between investment and speculation. It is true that speculation has been given a bad name—mainly by people who have been prudent enough as savers to acquire enough to invest but imprudent enough as investors to speculate when they thought they were investing. Just as speculation under the guise of investing begins by being imprudent and ends up by being unprofitable, so outright speculation, frankly recognized as such and within well-defined limits, has a minor role to play with the last "fling" of 5 to 10 percent availability of investment budgeting.

The budget which includes an investment program on a solid reserve of cash reserve, savings, and insurance and which develops a steady cash flow from the investment assets accumulated can set aside 5 to 10 percent of its investment availability for frank and outright speculation. I recommend that a speculating safety valve be opened for such flings, if only as insurance against the constant temptation of entrapment into speculation under the guise of investment.

Q. I am age 22, unmarried, with a salary of $11,000. Naturally, I don't know what the future holds, but I like to play the long shots. By the time I'm 40, my income could be 10 times what it is today. With this in mind, how much should I gamble on insurance?

Mr. P. T. (Boston, Massachusetts)

A. You're mixing horses and apples by speaking of gambling on insurance. It's the biggest bargain you can buy at your age, so long as you don't confuse it with investing. If you don't buy insurance now, one of the gambles you'll be making is that, despite your self-confidence, you'll not make yourself the luckiest man with the most wonderful woman in the world. Start out by buying $50,000 of straight life insurance now. If your confidence in your full earning power is justified, you'll want at least $250,000—assuming that in the meantime you will have built up investment assets along with your earning power. Just because you know enough about yourself to be clear that you are a long-shot player, my advice to you is to err on the long side in budgeting for insurance.

Q. I am 63 years old. My wife is 44, and we have two daughters, ages 14 and 12. My medical insurance is carried through my employer. When I retire, I will be covered by Medicare, but my wife and daughters will not. What would you advise?

Mr. P. H. (Greenville, South Carolina)

A. The problem you describe is real, and really trouble-some, for all married couples between whom there is any-thing like a 20-year discrepancy. As the older partner arrives at senior citizenhood, the urgent defense against the exposure you have identified is to do what is not on your mind; namely, buy life insurance.

I also suggest that your wife could help insure her future and make a better life for herself now by taking a job. This will kill two birds with one stone, if she can find one where the employer provides her and maybe even your daughters with health insurance. If not, she will have the extra money to buy it.

Q. I am 27, married, with one child. I am a geologist with an oil company which pays well, offers me a good future, and has excellent medical coverage, insurance, and profit-sharing programs. But I would like to invest in ad-ditional insurance for my family. Would you advise a straight life policy or an annuity?

Mr. J. M. B. (Houston, Texas)

A. Annuities are better for older people than for em-ployables just starting up. Your professional skill has landed you on the right side of the health-cost inflation, and you can safely anticipate steady increases in earned income. The most economic strategy you can follow, therefore, is to save for the present in order to put to-gether the wherewithal to invest in the future. Everyone should have insurance, and you can buy permanent insur-ance very cheaply at your age. But it is bad policy to confuse insurance with investment. Budget for insurance, and then concentrate on building a start-up investment "kitty."

Q. I am 24, one year out of college, married, with two children, and make $10,000 a year. We manage to put about $100 a month into savings. We rent our home. Although we have plans for many future purchases, we would like to start an investment program. What would you recommend?

Mr. W. J. (Wallace, Idaho)

A. I would recommend that you revise your thinking. I assume that you have already attended to your insurance obligation. Second only to reserved cash for an emergency, life insurance should be the top priority for any young family from the moment its first child is expected. Always buy insurance before beginning to invest. The younger anyone buying insurance is, the bigger the bargain is. The longer you wait, the more your insurance will cost you. Let your first proper investment be in a piece of land with a house on it. It will save you more and make you more than any plan for investing in securities.

Q. I have two $1,000 insurance policies that have been fully paid up for some years. The yearly dividends are nominal. I realize that the main feature of insurance is protection, and I have increased my protection with new policies when these matured. Wouldn't it be a better deal to take the cash surrender value (which is more than the amount paid in over the years) and put it into a mutual fund where it could grow and perhaps produce additional *income when I retire 12 years from now? The cash surrender value would only increase $100 or so in that time, and I'd probably lose more than that in purchasing power, should I cash them in then. Am I figuring this logically?*

Mrs. A. S. C. (Battle Creek, Michigan)

A. You answered your own question by stating that "the main feature of insurance is protection," and you have it. You are always protected so long as you pay each year's premium on your new policies.

I agree that you would be better off putting the money from your old policies to work for you. After all, your continuing commitment to insurance is buying you the freedom to invest. Use it.

Q. My wife and I are 45 years old. We recently inherited approximately $120,000, to be paid to us over the next three years. The first payment, due very soon, will be $25,000. This entire sum is free for investment. I am self-employed and have no retirement setup. Any suggestions would be appreciated.

Mr. R. S. B. (Detroit, Michigan)

A. Why don't you begin by buying straight life or term insurance to offset your lack of any retirement plan? You will have enough cash to meet premium costs comfortably by the time your $120,000 inheritance is paid to you in full. Investment values are likely to become real bargains, so don't let the first $25,000 burn a hole in your pocket. Put it in the bank, but don't let this much cash sit in your checking account earning no interest.

Q. I am 40, separated from my husband, and have two small children to support on my salary of $9,000. Because of the death of my uncle, I am to receive insurance amounting to $30,000. My two questions are: What kind of tax will I have to pay on the insurance? Should I take payment in one sum or in installments?

Mrs. E. P. C. (Memphis, Tennessee)

A. You need pay no tax if the insurance comes to you as a beneficiary on the death of an insured person. From a tax standpoint it makes no difference whether the insurance is paid to you in one sum or in installments.

By all means take your death benefits in one lump sum. With your two children and your low salary, you are on the spot to put the money to work earning as much extra income as possible. The faster you can have the use of the money, the better chance you will have to work out of the hole any woman in your position is bound to be in.

Q. We are a working couple, age 38, no children, living in an inexpensive apartment. We both do physical work, have only high school educations, and one is self-employed. Our combined income last year was $18,000. We have meager insurance, $15,000 in certificates of deposit at 5.4 percent, and $5,000 in volatile stocks, on which we have managed to glean a yearly profit averaging $1,000, with the help of a good broker and luck. Growth is our objective, but at this point I am in a quandary as to how to achieve it. Should we continue to speculate?

Mrs. B. H. (Cincinnati, Ohio)

A. Let me begin by answering the question you didn't ask. I don't think you have enough insurance. Each of you has been depending on the other's income. You'll do well to insure this state of affairs by taking out life insurance. While you're at it, get some medical and health insurance as well. This is particularly important for the self-employed, who forgo such fringe benefits enjoyed by organization men and women.

Answering your question about speculation, it seems to me that your luck is about to run out. Quit while you're ahead. In today's ticklish situation, people out to get growth will be doing very well if they stay even.

Q. I am 30, married, and have two children. My annual salary is $16,000. I am making the usual monthly payments on home mortgage, car, and insurance—as well as payments on a boat, a washing machine and a dryer, a color television set, a correspondence course in painting, and a fur coat for my wife. My life insurance policy is for $30,000. But considering the mortgage, on which I owe $24,000, my debts are $32,000—twice the amount of my annual income and $2,000 more than my insurance. If I were to die, what would happen?

Mr. R. P. C. (Boston, Massachusetts)

A. Your wife would have to go to work for that fur coat you bought her with what otherwise would have been your savings and insurance.

The fact that you are frightened enough to ask suggests that at least your subconscious is sensible enough to sound the alarm. Begin by selling your boat and canceling your correspondence course. Take what you can salvage from your floating folly, and put it into as much more insurance as it will buy for your family. Take the time you have been wasting on phony social prestige and figure out how to use it to earn some extra income.

Q. *I am an electrician, age 35, married, with three children. Over the past five years, my annual income has more than doubled, so that I now gross over $30,000. Naturally, I pay more taxes and have bought a second car and new furniture, as well as making larger mortgage payments on our new home. Otherwise our way of life is much the same as it was five years ago. Still, I'm no more able to put away any savings from $30,000 than when I was making $12,000. I don't believe my problem is entirely due to the rise in cost of living. Can you give me some advice?*

Mr. J. D. (Baltimore, Maryland)

A. I agree with you that your problem is not entirely due to the rise in the cost of living. In fact, I think you are more responsible for your problem than inflation is.

The cost of the manufactured products you are buying certainly has not gone up anything like 50 percent in the last five years. True, some services have, but I imagine that your family spends more on goods than on services. Moreover, your property tax payments are a more valuable tax deduction to you now than when you were making $12,000, and so are your interest payments on your mortgage.

I assume that your labor contract is giving you valuable fringe benefits in the form of health insurance. If you can't set aside cash for emergency reserves, and on top of that, cash for a savings reserve, on a $30,000 income,

I doubt that you would be able to do so on $40,000 or even $50,000.

Your problem is not financial. It is disciplinary. I suggest that you treat the cash you have been spending as a back debt involving the same kind of fixed obligation as you pay on your mortgage, and second only to it. You might tax yourself with a savings plan and bank the proceeds, keeping the change paid you as interest. You can use it.

CHAPTER III

Cash

NEVER before have so many ordinary people had so much money and been confronted with so many choices about how to put it to work.

The old outworn texts on economics assume that business has "cash" and the people who work for it and buy from it don't. Present-day realities have reversed this rule, along with so many others.

The bigger the money-users are nowadays, the more anxiously they are looking for cash to borrow. It is mainly families, rather than businesses, that have cash to lend—as well as access to the sole form of borrowed "cash" readily available today, credit-card "cash." Businesses have become the new poor, and their employees the new rich. "What can you do with cash?" used to be a popular refrain in business circles. Now business is finding out how hard it is to get along without it.

"Cash" is usable spending power. To begin with, it is money—dollar bills and checking accounts. But spending power, ready to be used when and as needed, can also be held in what the trade calls "cash equivalents." The main categories of these are savings deposits, time deposits, Treasury bills, and commercial paper. There are also credit cards, the newest form of cash equivalent.

Each type of cash equivalent has emerged in response to the needs of a particular sort of money-user: savings deposits, for example, are where the little fellow or the consumer keeps his cash; commercial paper was where big cash holdings could be put to work for short hauls.

When money-users keep their spending power in cash equivalents rather than in the sock under the bed, the cash they will spend tomorrow is available for someone else to spend today. Therefore, cash equivalents earn interest for their owner. The spread between interest rates on different kinds of cash and cash equivalents reflects the relative ease with which they can actually be used to make purchases in the market place. Dollar bills and checking accounts earn no interest—they are available to the owner instantaneously. The longer the owner sacrifices the use of his cash, the more interest he will earn on it. The exception is the user of credit-card "cash" who is expected to pay for the privilege like any other borrower.

The increasing demand for cash has resulted in a rapid rise in interest rates. The big money-users have become so desperate for cash, and are willing to pay so much for it, that the price for its hire has risen even faster than the price of hiring labor.

Long before the "hard hats" in the construction unions began to see doubles in their pay rates, cash had doubled its earnings. And while construction workers have pushed up their rates in part to offset the loss of overtime, the take-home pay of cash-holders has soared because the demand for their money has soared.

The reversal of roles in the market for cash, and its expensive consequences, saw its beginning in 1968 and 1969. Before President Nixon formulated his political appeal to the silent majority, the inflation in the economy and the deflation in the stock market demonstrated that a silent majority was in action in the market place.

Up and down the Main Streets of America, the members of this silent majority were quietly getting their cash together and putting it out to hire at higher and higher rates.

Suddenly the sophisticates on Wall Street have found themselves stranded with only each other to sell to, while the millions of commonsensical amateurs who have succeeded in accumulating billions of dollars now face the problem of how best to put their money to work— how to keep what they have and make more.

Here are typical questions from Main Street about cash and its uses. Here are the answers differentiating between various forms of cash itself, cash equivalents, and the various investment uses to which cash can be put.

Q. I'm a taxicab driver, married, age 45. I've worked hard all my life, but I've never been ahead of the game. Right now, all I have to spare is a pocketful of quarter tips. Any suggestions?

Mr. S. J. (Detroit, Michigan)

A. Count your blessings. In this topsy-turvy world, inflation has played one of its characteristic "now-you-see-it—now-you-don't" tricks with coin. It is true that everything costs so much nowadays that paper has out-grown silver just as prices have outgrown coin. But it is also true that we live in a "keep the change" economy. Anyone breaking a bill (all the way from $1 up to $100) is increasingly inclined to be casual about the change. Your customers' problem in keeping track of it (or even bothering with it at all) is your opportunity.

Ask any neighborhood branch bank for a coin box or piggy bank. If you are conscientious about saving your tips, you'll be surprised at how fast the piggy bank will fill up and build to dollar equivalents. The better-run local governments in the United States are becoming in-creasingly coin conscious—as is shown by their concern in skimming sales-tax coin receipts off the top of the con-sumer-spending stream. What's good enough for City Hall will be worthwhile for you. The more casual the suckers become about their loose change, the more they will toss your way. Grab it and let it build up for you.

Q. My husband and I have been married six months. Our only quarrel has been about our joint checking account, which my husband recently changed from a regular checking account to a charter check credit account. As I understand it, we can overdraw our account up to $1,000, but the annual compound interest on the overdraft is 12.17 percent! Since we have a savings account which we can borrow from, it seems to me ridiculous to borrow and pay such high interest charges. My husband says that borrowing on this checking account is a good thing because it establishes a line of credit. Which of us is right?

Mrs. R. B. C. (St. Louis, Missouri)

A. Your savings account establishes your credit. I think your family argument is confusing the purpose of a checking account, which is to pay bills, with a savings account, which is to help you get ahead of the game.

There are three kinds of checking accounts: (1) The special checking account which averages a small balance. On this type of account, 10¢ is charged for each check written, and there is a small monthly carrying charge. (2) The regular checking account on which there is no service charge if a minimum balance is maintained. The balance varies with the bank. It may be as low as $300 or as high as $800. (3) The charter checking account which allows overdrafts up to a specified amount. Obviously, an overdraft is a loan, and banks charge interest on loans. If you need to borrow, offer to pay the going rate. The rate you are paying is in line with that being borne by the best corporations in the world.

It is a form of being penny-wise and pound-foolish to get ahead of yourself building a savings account, while running short and borrowing in your checking account.

Q. I am 14. By the end of the summer I will have earned about $1,000 from baby-sitting. I want to save this money and to earn enough more so that when I am 16 I can go to New York City and study ballet. I am not interested in any investment risks but, because my uncle has been telling me about inflation, I am worried about putting my money in a savings bank. (I can't keep it at home because one of my brothers, who doesn't work, is likely to borrow it without returning it.)

My uncle says that if I take my $1,000 and put it into a savings bank, which pays 5 percent interest, I will have

$1,050 at the end of the year. But inflation is eroding the value of my money at 8 percent, so that instead of making $50, I am really losing $30. On top of it all, I'm expected to pay income tax! What should I do?

Miss K. T. M. (Pine Mountain, Georgia)

A. I truly sympathize. You are being exposed to the harsh inequities of inflation and taxation at an early age—but better early than too late. Although your uncle is right about inflation eroding the value of money, you most certainly will do better putting your money in a savings bank. There it is not only safe from borrowing brothers, but it *is* paying you 5 percent, which is, after all, better than the nothing it would earn if hidden at home.

I believe that, despite inflation, everyone has an economic use for a savings account as a cash reserve for emergencies and as a way to earn a modest return while accumulating cash for big, once-a-year expenditures. It is also a good way for young people like you to build up enough money to invest in your future.

Savers will always fall behind in the inflationary rat race so long as it is on. How investors can stay even with it, or move ahead of it, is the broader purpose of this book.

Q. Please explain what a United States Treasury bill is. Is it risky? Or is it covered by some form of United States insurance? Would you recommend it as an investment?

Miss C. V. (Denver, Colorado)

A. A Treasury bill is a short-term debt instrument, ranging up to one year: but most bills are issued with maturities of 90 or 180 days; 9-month and 12-month bills are also available. The Treasury sells its bills as often and as fast as it needs money. Treasury bills are not investment securities. They are interest-bearing cash equivalents.

It would be pointless for the Treasury to insure its own debt because it would have to issue the paper to make good its own default. As a practical matter, all Treasury paper is "money-good." The investor can count on getting his interest and the face amount of the bill promptly at maturity. If he needs his money before the bill comes due, he can sell it for cash without any loss of interest, which is pro-rated on a daily basis.

Although Treasury bills are fashionable with a host of amateur savers, they are not a medium for either savings or investment. They represent a way of holding cash at short term and getting paid for it. When interest rates are high, Treasury bills pay a higher rate of return than savings accounts.

Q. I understand that Treasury bills are no longer issued in denominations less than $10,000. Is this not depriving the Treasury of a big market for the paper it is constantly trying to sell, as well as penalizing the small saver?

Mr. E. O. J. (Akron, Ohio)

A. The reason the minimum was raised to $10,000 is that the Government was being embarrassed by the rate at which small savers were pulling cash out of savings accounts in order to buy bills—forcing the Treasury to sell bonds at still higher rates to advance back to the savings institutions to keep them going.

The answer to your second question is yes. Corporations—notably A.T.&T., which is the biggest of them—are doing a better job of selling to the small saver than the Government is. But, even now, when Government, business, and banks are competing to attract savers' money, I have not heard of anyone going out of his way to give the small saver a break.

Q. I am a widow, age 78, and in fine health. I have $50,000 in certificates of deposit and will soon receive $10,000 from the sale of my house. I'm afraid of brokers, but I wonder if I don't have too much money in certificates of deposit?

Mrs. L. G. (Pompano Beach, Florida)

A. Your problem is that you have confused cash with investment. It makes no sense for any individual in your circumstances to freeze so much money in certificates of deposit, which are useful either as a way to hold cash reserves or to save up investment availability.

Certificates of deposit are cash equivalents, not as readily usable as demand deposits in checking accounts and tying up larger sums than are insured by banks in savings accounts. Like deposits in savings accounts, certificates of deposit are time deposits—that is, they pay interest at a fixed rate over a stipulated number of months. Interest rates on certificates of deposit do *not* fluctuate with money market conditions as Treasury bills do. They are mainly for businesses and businessmen needing to negotiate bank loans and under pressure, literally, to "buy" credit from banks by putting up deposits.

I can understand your not trusting brokers to pick stocks for you. But it is almost impossible for them to go wrong in the selection of "good name" bonds which will earn you a much higher return than certificates of deposit. The trick is to prevent brokers from talking you into buying stocks for higher commissions.

Q. What on earth is "commercial paper?" I can't find it in the dictionary, but my brother-in-law talks about it all the time.

Mrs. H. W. (Waco, Texas)

A. I hope your brother-in-law has a more comprehensive dictionary and knows what he's talking about. "Commercial paper" is money market lingo for short-term, unsecured promissory notes issued by top-rated businesses and by bank borrowers with cash or verified bank loans equal to their borrowings. Presumably, therefore, they do not really need to borrow, but are using their presumed financial strength to take advantage of a money market bargain.

But the old idea that borrowers prefer this kind of borrowing to bank loans has gone the way of other intellectual casualties of the present credit crunch. Many big borrowers have been resorting to commercial paper as an emergency substitute for bank loans, which their banks are obligated to make but can't. Worse still, they are promising to repay this short-term money with bank borrowings—on the theory that the banks will be free to service their customers again in a matter of months.

The best credit risks in the world do not normally operate with postdated checks. The fact that they are forced to resort to this dubious practice, and that their banks know it and have no alternative but to encourage it, suggests that the bulge in the commercial paper float measures the severity of the present credit crisis. The Penn Central bankruptcy left no doubt how risky indiscriminate I.O.U.-printing can be when not backed up by usable lines of bank credit. The tip as to the timing of bankruptcy came when Penn Central lost the "prime" rating that is a business borrower's passport to the commercial paper market. Bankruptcy followed in a matter of days.

As a practical matter, the commercial paper of the very best-rated corporations and banks is a safe enough way to hold cash equivalents whenever interest rates are high. The normal holding period is anything from 27 days to a year, and the rate is generally a point or so above that of Treasury bills. The minimum amount for purchasing commercial paper is usually $100,000. Only when money is tight and expensive can it be bought for as little as $25,000. Commercial paper is for larger cash-users who are presumed to be sophisticated enough to gauge risks. The higher interest rates go, the riskier it is to buy commercial paper from any except the best of names.

Q. My husband is 52, I am 50, and our children are grown. Our combined salaries average $12,000 a year; but my husband's company is having management trouble, and we may have to seek new employment. We are reevaluating our financial situation and would like your advice. We have adequate insurance. Our home, valued *at $20,000, is paid for. We have $14,750 in a certificate of deposit, $1,250 in Government bonds and $3,000 in auto stock. We are mainly concerned with retirement income and would like to invest in something. What would you suggest?*

Mrs. K. B. (Enid, Oklahoma)

A. Most companies which have awakened to discover that they are having management trouble are on the verge of discovering that they are having money trouble, too. No time is a good time to have either management or money trouble, but today is the very worst time. Consequently, until your husband can again feel secure about his earned income, your best bet is to regard the substantial *cash reserve* you have accumulated as just that—*not* as an investment kitty. (This policy also suggests the prudence of your liquidating the $3,000 in auto stock holdings, without regard to their investment merits. You cannot afford to freeze your savings in them.)

Everyone with reason to worry about job shifting needs a cash reserve. No one with cash reserve problems is ready to begin investment.

Q. I have received a settlement of $210,000 from an accident. As a result of the accident, I have lost an arm and will be confined to a wheelchair for the rest of my life. After payment of legal fees and settlement of some personal debts, I will have about $125,000. I am 45 years old, divorced, and have no assets other than this money. Since it is doubtful if I will be able to work again, and I am afraid I may have additional medical expenses in the future, I would appreciate your advice on what to do with *this money which will have to take care of me for the rest of my life.*

Mr. J. L. D. (Roanoke, Virginia)

A. You clearly cannot afford to live on capital, because your disability has deprived you of your earning power. I think you are realistic in assuming you will have additional medical expenses to absorb. In view of the runaway increases in health costs, I think it will be prudent to segregate no less than $25,000 of your capital in cash savings accounts, accepting the lower interest. In your circumstances, you need to count on ready accessibility to cash.

Count yourself lucky (in spite of your tragic circumstances) that bond yields have doubled during these years of money trouble. Good corporation bonds will pay close to 10 percent, guaranteeing you, meanwhile, against their being called and being refunded with lower-yielding instruments if—and I think it likely—interest rates should fall during the period that the non-call provision is in effect.

Of course, if I am right in expecting interest rates to fall within the next ten years, bonds bought now will go to a premium and be salable at a profit. Also, stocks will be safe to own again for investors in your circumstances, who are dependent upon income and cannot afford to risk capital.

I assume you will be able to manage on the 10 percent income from $100,000 invested in bonds and with the 5 percent-plus interest from your $25,000 savings paying for extras.

Q. Recently my 15-year-old son received unsolicited through the mail a Bank Americard. My 23-year-old son, who is employed and has had a checking account for several years, applied for a Bank Americard. His application was turned down because he did not have sufficient credit rating. The whole system seems crazy to me. What good are bank credit cards, anyway?

Mr. S. P. (New York, New York)

A. I agree with you that the system is crazy. Bank retail credit cards are a prime example of credit being proliferated without restraint or extra supervision at a time when banks themselves have been hard put to raise overnight loans to meet their old commitments. Logic will be defied, and so will sound financial practice, so long as banks offer unsecured term loans to the public at large—which is what mass credit card distribution amounts to—at a time when they can't meet their loan commitments to their own business borrowers.

Fortunately, state legislatures in New York, Massachusetts, and elsewhere have now passed bills outlawing the issuance of credit cards to people who do not request them. Parallel Federal legislation is pending.

Bank retail cards, such as Bank Americard, Uni-Serve, and Master Charge, do serve the purpose of allowing those who have them to charge purchases in small retail stores that do not have their own billing system. The stores pay the service charge, which may run as high as 7 percent. The customer who uses a bank retail card need not pay the interest charge, usually 1½ percent, if the bill is paid within thirty days.

My advice to your older son is to open charge accounts

at several large department stores. Then he can establish a credit rating and get a retail bank credit card. My advice to your son is also that this is one game it is good sound business to beat, and that he is not too young to sharpen his pencil and learn how to do it. The legitimate way to beat it is to use the 25-day grace period before interest accumulates on outstanding balances as just that—an interest-free grace period and no more. Be sure to alert him against being suckered into the bank credit merchandisers' gimmick, which requires payment on only a minimum portion of the outstanding balance. The game the bank plays is to test the sucker public's credit while encouraging it to contribute to bank earnings at 1½ percent a month (or 18 percent a year). Explain to your son that it will pay him to charge no more than he can pay for *in full* in 25 days and to pay up in full.

Q. I know the puritan virtues are out of fashion now. But I still don't like the notion of going into debt. Since borrowing seems to be the only way of establishing credit, can you explain to me why—if I have the cash—credit is so important?

Mr. A. L. (Portland, Maine)

A. In this day and age the old adage that no man's credit is as good as his cash is baloney. With alarming rises in crime and increased personal anonymity, especially in the large urban areas, anyone walking around with large sums of cash today is a likely candidate for a blow on the head and an empty pocket. If such an unpleasant event did occur, and the victim needed hospital care, unfortunately it would be necessary for him to prove his ability to pay. On weekends, when banks aren't open, a millionaire who can't prove he is good for $10 is just another vagrant. Not even the admitting offices of city hospitals operate as humanitarian institutions nowadays. A credit card is a money-good passport to guaranteeing entitlement to emergency services. Credit is not only as good as—but very often it is better than—cash.

As to your opinion of borrowing, if inflation continues to speed up, anyone interested enough in the old-fashioned puritan virtues can make more money borrowing than working. The recipe for doing so is to pay back dollars borrowed today with dollars worth less tomorrow. Anyone with cash can be sure of playing this game without running the familiar borrowers' risk of getting overextended.

Q. I was brought up always to pay cash on the line for everything I could afford. Is there any reason why I should use credit cards?

Mr. A. D. (Concord, New Hampshire)

A. You were brought up right. The worst danger for a family is extending the use of credit from where it is necessary and appropriate—as in buying a car or a house —to areas where it is not appropriate. Credit cards for business expenses do make sense: they give a valid record of tax-deductible spending. Even bank credit cards can make sense for a prudent man or woman. Possession of one can be the only means of obtaining emergency services on a money-down basis—whether for your car or for yourself, for example, in case of accident. If you do have a bank credit card, be aware of the charge structure: 1½ percent per month on the outstanding balance. The issuer wants the balance to be outstanding and to collect the interest rate at 18 percent per year. You can stay ahead of the credit card game by paying your outstanding balance on the 25th day after the billing date. That way you escape all finance charges and have at least 25 days of credit, interest-free.

CHAPTER IV

Property

THROUGH the years, property has been the first *bona-fide* investment that folks make—after saving up enough to provide themselves with a cash reserve and covering their families with adequate insurance. It has come first as an investment because America has been a land of home-owners; land, and the family home on it, are the most basic forms of property investment.

In times when rents accelerate beyond the ability of families to hold them down to 25 percent of net usable income, investing in property—outside of rent-controlled New York—represents the profitable way to play the game. The inflation in property values is the other side of the coin from the inflation in rent costs.

For a relatively small outlay an ordinary family can enjoy the use of assets with many times its actual cash commitment. The interest portion of its payments is tax-deductible, and the mortgage itself is seen to be a big plus to the borrower if he wants to sell his house. As interest rates rise, a house is easier to sell if it was mortgaged when interest rates were lower. A mortgage also helps to set a value on the house.

At the other end of the scale, the Church of England and the late Ambassador Joseph P. Kennedy, the perspicacious and very rich Founding Father of the Kennedy clan, provide proof of the rewards that big-time property investment can bring. The Church of England was the first institutional investor in land and, over the years, its position as Britain's biggest and richest landlord, outside of the Crown, has been its main source of wealth and power. Incidentally, but not accidentally, the Church of England was also the British originator of the "cult of the equity" —that is, investment in stocks as the way to invest in growth and to hedge against inflation (at least for a time); the Church of England has demonstrated that investment in property and investment in the stock market, far from being mutually exclusive, can both be used with discriminating selectivity by professional management. Joe Kennedy made his first stake going short against the stock market before the 1929 bust. After that, he remained continuously bearish on stocks, and put his chips back in property, becoming one of the richest men in the world.

Over the years more money is made Church-of-England-and-Joe-Kennedy style than in chasing stocks and securities. Moreover, more people who could not afford the cost of investment advice when it was cheaper and safer have made more money on owning their own homes than they have lost in securities.

In time of inflation, property is a particularly attractive investment for two special reasons. The first is that good buildings—from family homes to skyscrapers—and the land they stand on become scarce when accelerating inflation drives interest rates up and makes credit tight. Meanwhile, however, the same acceleration in inflation increases incomes at the very time when the drying up of credit prevents the financing of new construction. When more money chases the same number of places to live, popular-priced real estate values and rents rise. The old saw about land—it's the best investment around, because the government can't print it—holds equally good for buildings.

Secondly, inflation makes property investment wise investment because of the premium it puts on owing money rather than on being owed it. Real estate in all its forms can be used as a vehicle enabling investors to buy inflation insurance with the money they owe on mortgages which they will pay back in depreciated dollars. What's more, borrowing on property is a way to reduce risks because the property, in effect, owes the money. The more professional the real estate borrower, the more certain it is that the owner is not the ower, although the law can play its part here, too, and it varies from state to state. In some states the borrowers' other assets or income can be attached in default of mortgage payments; in others, like New York, they cannot.

Sociologically speaking, most people who buy securities do not understand real property, and most people who buy real property do not understand securities. But the property market offers the investor as wide a variety of places to put his money as does the securities market— from undeveloped land or land rich in natural resources (like timber and oil) through one-family homes to apartment and office buildings, and on to major development projects.

Once the step is made to contemplate property as a commercial investment—and to go beyond mortgaging the family home—investors in property are on notice to recognize the same injunctions as investors in stocks. Aside from raw, undeveloped land, held for eventual resale, property requires professional management on a day-to-day basis. Managerial expertise and experience can be bought. It can also be learned, often with greater profit. But, just as the returns from professional investment in property can dwarf those available in the securities markets, and at far less risk, so the rule of prudence is to be observed throughout: the commitment to invest commands a continuing commitment, paid for in dollars or in time and never without risk, to manage the investment. Also, when investing in any kind of property, whether it's the family home or an apartment building, it is of prime importance to see that it is fully insured. I have known professional investors who have had a building burn down on them, only to find it was not covered by fire insurance.

An increasingly popular form of property investment is the sale and leaseback arrangement in which the owner of a piece of property sells it to a person or group of people and simultaneously leases it back from them. The advantage for the seller in this transaction is that he receives a lump sum of money for ready use, probably taking a profit on what he paid for the property originally. The rent he has to pay is fixed at the time the agreement is made. The buyers, on the other hand, have all the advantages of property ownership—the tax benefits in particular—plus the possibility of participating in a future capital gain on resale. The size of the commitment generally needed to participate in a sale-leaseback limits access to this particularly attractive form of property investment.

Tax considerations are a critical factor in property investment. Property owners are entitled to apply the annual depreciation in the value of the property they own to reduce their taxable income. Income earned from the property can thus be "sheltered," and there can also be a "spill-over" to shelter a portion of other income, too. The new Tax Reform Act of 1969, however, serves notice that hoggish attempts to accelerate depreciation unduly can jeopardize legitimate tax shelters. Since the interest owed on a mortgage is deductible from income, property owners can also gain tax advantages from property investment by prepaying interest and gaining a lump-sum deduction; although the 1969 Tax Act restricts this "gimmicky" incentive to property ownership, too. A third tax consideration in property investment is that some income received from property can be treated as a repayment of the original capital invested; when the property is sold, however, taxable capital gains include the full difference between the price received and the *reduced* original cost.

The complicated tax regulations affecting property ownership mean that experienced professional advice is a "must" for the uninitiated investor. On-the-job training in the rules and opportunities can produce greater—and safer—rewards for investors willing to spend the time and able to put up the money than any other investment program. For the small investor, real estate investment trusts are as yet the sole public vehicle aside from the stocks of property development companies, which have all the volatility of stock market investment.

While real estate investment trusts do allow the small investor to get a piece of the action under the aegis of professional management, they also have three big limitations. First, in order to pass on the tax shelter they enjoy to investors, they are required to pay out at least 90 percent of their income in dividends; this means that they are unable to build up internal resources for further investment. Consequently, real estate trusts, once they are fully invested, are chronically illiquid, having to go back to the public or sell off existing assets whenever new money is required.

Second, real estate investment trusts are restricted to owning property: they are not allowed to manage it. Finally, the "leverage" which they can gain by borrowing money to boost their investing power is also restricted. The large equity positions they are required to take in their assets makes them vulnerable any time one of their properties goes bad, which is always a possibility.

Real estate investment trusts, thus, are not ideal vehicles for property investment. They do offer the higher-bracket taxpayer, interested primarily in income, some of the tax advantages of investing in property. But for the investor willing and able to set aside enough to make a meaningful start-up commitment, his own money, leveraged with a mortgage, can get him into property without the limitations imposed on the investment trusts. He is on special notice, however, in this complex area, to pay the additional price of obtaining the professional guidance needed to prevent an investment opportunity from becoming an investor's disaster.

The one new and attractive way to avoid this problem is to invest in property mutual funds—which I believe will fulfill a long-felt want. They are the coming thing both in the mutual fund business and in the property management and investment business.

Q. We are part of the unfortunate middle class: not wealthy enough to afford living in today's inflationary period, and not poor enough to receive government aid. My mother, a widow, and I live together in an apartment. I earn a good salary, but we occasionally need to dip into our meager savings to meet expenses. We have adequate insurance, and I have 1,200 shares of a mutual fund. We will collect some money from a debt in the near future, and I would like to know how best to invest it. We need security, growth, and income—a large order. Since I am middle-aged, I feel I don't have too much time to accomplish this. Should we use our money to make a down payment on a condominium?

Miss D. D. (Lansing, Michigan)

A. I feel for you. If the beginning of wisdom is to know your problem, you have achieved it. Home ownership offers you your best chance of getting your own back —certainly more so than if you continue to live on the wrong side of the landlord-tenant relationship. Whether you should go for a condominium or a home depends on local conditions. Ask your bank at least to direct you to one of the real estate firms it deals with.

Q. Some time ago, we purchased a home for $21,000 with a $14,000 mortgage at 5¾ percent interest. It has been my plan to pay off my present mortgage as soon as possible and use the increased equity as a down payment on

*a larger home. I know you disapprove of paying off mort-
gages, but what else would you suggest I do with the
approximately $250 per month I have available for this
purpose?*

Mr. J. J. L. (Villa Park, Illinois)

A. Don't yield to temptation. Don't prepay your mortgage. Keep making your regular payments, but put your
extra cash into bonds yielding 8 percent or better. If you
want to sell your house, a mortgage at even higher than
5¾ percent is a tremendous sales asset in the market in
which sellers will be hard-pressed to find buyers able to
finance purchase prices. A 5¾ percent mortgage rate is a
real bargain today, not least because back when mortgages still cost only 5¾ percent payback terms were longer
and the payback money (or, as it's called, amortization)
is more expensive to the mortgage borrower than interest
charges because it is not tax-deductible. It's a safe rule
never to give a bargain away.

*Q. I paid $10,000 for my house but now believe it
could be worth as much as $25,000. My wife and I are
both in our late fifties and we have been talking about
moving to a smaller place in the country, since our children have grown up and left home. Will I have to pay
capital gains tax on any profit I make on selling our present home?*

Mr. S. T. B. (Los Angeles, California)

A. If you buy yourself a new house and start living
in it within a year either before or after the sale, you
avoid paying tax on all the proceeds so long as your new

home costs at least as much as the price you receive for the old one. But if it costs *less*, then you are liable to pay tax on the difference. The same rule applies if you decide to build a home, although then you are given an 18-month grace period after the sale within which to start living in it. Any capital expenditure on the building during the year before and the 18-month grace period is taken into account in assessing the cost of the house.

Remember, however, that whether buying or building, you have just postponed your liability, and if you later decide to sell the new house, you will be confronted with a tax demand based on the original price of the old one.

There is one big exception to all this, but it will only apply to you if for some reason you decide to postpone selling your home until you are 65. Anyone aged 65 or over who sells his house is allowed $20,000 of the money from the sale free of capital gains tax, as long as he has lived in the house for five years during an eight-year period before the sale.

Q. You recently advised a widow that the money she could generate by mortgaging her home could be put to work to contribute substantially toward her need. I can't see how. I'm 61, retired, and own my home outright. Assuming that I can mortgage my house for $15,000, exactly how could I use the money profitably—a safe investment which would enable me to pay off the mortgage at the present high interest rate and still show a gain.

Mr. J. W. H. (Downers Grove, Illinois)

A. The problem presented by your complaint about high interest rates is as long as it is broad. Granted that the money you would raise on your mortgage would cost you a high rate, it would also bring you a high return. The mortgage you would get would give you long-term money; the longer the term, the lower the annual rate of payback, despite the high rate of interest.

You can bank the certainty that five years from now, let alone 15 years from now, the money you will be paying back to the lender each year will be worth a lot less than the money the lender will be giving you this year. Over the span of the next 5-15 years, sound investments will be worth substantially more than what $15,000 of investable cash is worth today, and meanwhile they will be paying for themselves in rates of return that have been inflated as much as the cost of borrowing on mortgages. How and where you could put the money to work to best advantage depends on your tax bracket, amount of earned income, other resources, and so on. Calculations about the cost of money and the return on it necessarily need to be adjusted to allow for the tax factor. Anyone with enough money to worry about the cost of borrowing and the return on investing the proceeds of borrowing is undoubtedly a taxpayer. Taking the 50 percent tax bracket as representative, a mortgage borrower paying as high as 10 percent is incurring a net after-tax cost of 5 percent. As to whether this pays, the fact that top-quality medium-term tax-exempt bonds have been going begging at net tax-free yields of up to 7½ percent leaves no doubt that it does. For the post-tax value of tax-exempts to taxpayers in the 50 percent bracket see Chapter VIII on bonds.

Q. I am a 72-year-old professional man, my wife is 67, and we have no dependents. We plan to retire next year.

We both have Medicare coverage plus extra protection and adequate life insurance. Income from interest and Social Security will be about $9,000 annually. I have $87,000 invested chiefly in bonds paying 6 to 7 percent, and $2,000 in certificates of deposit. My wife also has $2,000 in a savings account.

When we retire, I plan to build a home at a cost of $20,000 to $22,000. You have advised others to keep a mortgage on a home rather than buy outright. Do you think it would be wise for me to borrow part or all when I build, rather than cash some of the bonds, when they mature next year?

Mr. K. K. E. (Bloomington, Wisconsin)

A. Absolutely—especially in your circumstances, because of your high, unearned taxable income, and also because your savings are invested in bonds. You need all the deductions you can get in the form of interest expense; also, the appreciation on your new home will be a useful hedge against inflation. The fact that only private persons prudent enough to make themselves cash-rich in the continuing emergency can afford to build their own homes leaves no doubt that homes built now will be worth much more later.

Q. I am 57 and will be retiring in eight years. At present my wife and I rent a quiet duplex for $100 a month. Would I be further ahead by continuing as is, or putting $1,000 down on buying a house which we would plan to sell when I retire?

Mr. L. F. S. (Detroit, Michigan)

A. Sounds to me like your rent is a real bargain. Sit tight, but make sure you are protected by a lease, because rents are headed up. New building is lagging, and landlords will be able to pass their higher costs on to tenants. Although home ownership becomes a more expensive proposition when building costs and interest rates rise, rents for most tenants have been literally going through the roof, so that home ownership is still relatively more attractive. You, however, are ahead of the landlord-tenant game; if you can stay ahead, do so. What's more, you can't buy much of a house nowadays with $1,000 down.

Q. *If you had $100,000 to invest and you wanted to guard yourself against inflation, knowing full well if you lost it there would be no way to recover due to old age, what would you do? Would you invest in vacant property, income property, stocks, bonds, tax-exempt bonds, savings and loan associations, bank stocks, foreign exchange, or leave it in cash or what? I took quite a loss in 1929 and I'm trying to avoid a repeat performance.*

Mr. W. K. E. (*Glenview, Illinois*)

A. Sounds to me like you've been running over-scared during all the years since the last crash and are getting your nerve back just when it's time to get scared again. My first vote goes to income-producing property, financed on long-term mortgages. But don't go overboard and leave yourself cash-short.

Q. *In a recent column you commented that there wasn't much sense in owning income property without a mortgage, because money borrowed now could be paid* *back later in much cheaper dollars. Does that mean that, if the price of gold should go to $70 an ounce, I could pay off my $20,000 mortgage for only $10,000? When you said "much cheaper money," did you mean this much cheaper? Surely lending institutions must have some provision in loan contracts to guard against this sort of charity to their customers.*

Mr. T. Z. (Cincinnati, Ohio)

A. My advice to put long-term mortgages on property would work out profitably no matter what happens to the price of gold—even if it falls as the result of being entirely demonetized—so long as the domestic purchasing power of the dollar continues to shrink. Mortgage owners are obligated to pay back the same number of dollars they borrow—plus interest, of course. But the fact that the purchasing power of those dollars at the retail counter is expected to be worth less when the time comes to pay them back creates the incentive to borrow against property now. Over the span of the next couple of decades, I certainly do expect the purchasing power of the dollar to fall by another 50 percent.

Your common-sense concern for the cost of inflation to people owed fixed-interest obligations, like mortgage lending institutions, does you credit. Many realistic thinkers in this field are intrigued with the possibilities of what might be called a variable mortgage. The borrower would pay a fixed number of dollars each month, and the portion allocated between interest and amortization would vary with the interest rate. Automatic adjustments in the interest rate would work out equitably for both sides of the deal over a period of time.

Q. I am 26 years old, with an annual income of $10,000. I am considering purchasing a six-year-old two-flat brick apartment building costing $28,000 with an income of $3,000 per year. Wouldn't this be better than investing in mutual funds, of which I know nothing?

Mr. R. F. R. (South Holland, Illinois)

A. I agree that you will probably do better with your apartment building project than in a mutual fund—provided, of course, that you know what you are doing in real estate and that the rental income is trustworthy. If you can get yourself any kind of mortgage, you will have a pretty fair yield. Also, the 1969-1970 slowdown in new residential construction is bound to be helpful to the market value of existing property.

Q. My wife and I recently bought an apartment building with a long-term mortgage to beat inflation. Our problem now is what to do with the extra income over mortgage payments and expenses. We can prepay the loan without penalty, but that would defeat the purpose of the long-term mortgage. Should we put the income into savings, or bonds, or buy stocks for the long pull?

Mr. D. S. J. (Cincinnati, Ohio)

A. Glad to see that you have the formula figured out. Glad to see, too, that you've been smart enough to make your use of debt pay you more in running income than it is costing. The last thing to do is to prepay the loan. I suggest that you let your operating profit build up in a savings account until you have a nest egg big enough to do something with—like buying another building.

Q. I am 72 years of age and in good health despite one heart attack. So is my 55-year-old wife, who is employable as a medical technician but has not—at least not yet—gone back to work. We have taken big paper losses in the stock market, although we own good stocks and our dividend income is holding up. Our one luxury, which I call my "floating rest-cure," is our $20,000 boat. We have no insurance and I am obviously uninsurable. Our home is worth somewhere in the neighborhood of $50,000, and there is $4,000 left to pay on our mortgage. Would you advise resetting the mortgage at a higher rate of interest and incurring monthly payment costs or letting it run off on schedule?

Mr. J. V. F. (Daytona Beach, Florida)

A. In your circumstances the best thing to do is to pay it off on schedule. Current income is what matters to you now, not accumulated capital gains for the future. The "swing" item in your family budget seems to be the monthly cost of your mortgage.

Q. I am 42, my wife is 39, and we have eight children aged one through 13. I am a city fireman earning $150 weekly net, which is just barely enough for living expenses. Fortunately, we own our home, which is worth about $15,000. We have $6,000 in savings, which was left last year by my mother. I would like to buy income property, preferably something we could also live in. Do you think it would be a good idea?

Mr. F. M. (Detroit, Michigan)

A. I would agree with your expression of preference for investment in income-producing property in which your family could also live. Income property in the price range you could afford does not lend itself to successful absentee management. It would seem to me that the $15,000 from the sale of your present home might go pretty far toward enabling you to buy a two-family dwelling from which the rent would help to service the mortgage. If I were you, I would not commit any of my cash reserve to such a venture. You will do well to remember that buying a house and fixing it up—especially for a tenant—eats up a lot of cash. Also, you will need all the cash you can set aside to keep up with the education and health bills waiting for you.

Q. *My wife and I are both over 65 and own income property, mortgage-free, which provides us with a very comfortable income. Due to inflation moves, would you advise selling this property now and putting the money in the bank? Or should we retain it and hope for the best?*

Mr. P. K. (Chicago, Illinois)

A. By all means, hold your property. But what is the sense of owning it without a mortgage? If your fear of inflation became a reality, you would pay back any dollars borrowed today in much cheaper money. The more stocks decline—and you have been righter than you have suspected—the more it will pay anyone with your income to owe money on income-producing property.

Q. *We own income-producing property, mortgage-free. Why is it better, as you often say, to carry a mort-*

*gage at 6 or 6½ percent when the money could earn a
return of only about 5 or 5½ percent?*

Mrs. G. M. (*Cincinnati, Ohio*)

A. If what is worrying you is the cost of servicing a
6 or 6½ percent mortgage, it no longer is any trick to earn
6 percent-plus on a bond. The mortgage interest cost is
tax deductible, and people in higher brackets and/or with
business operating deductions can earn substantially
higher after-tax yields than the after-tax cost of 6½ percent money.

Given the prospect for continued inflation of costs and
continued deflation of earnings, the long-term incentive
for mortgaging is to pay off debt in cheaper dollars; and
the short-term incentive is to have cash available for other
investments when bargain day arrives. The emergency
incentive is that a mortgage makes a house easier to sell
and at a good price.

*Q. I am 60 years old and have my own business, which
has made a comfortable living for my family in the last
30 years. We have $15,000 in a mutual fund, plus the busi-
ness—its land, building, and equipment—which has a book
value of $130,000. We recently sold our home and ob-
tained $10,000 equity from it; we now rent an apartment.
Should I sell the business and hold onto the real estate,
or sell both and invest the proceeds in the fund? Where
should we invest the money from our home?*

Mr. B. M. (*Fort Lauderdale, Florida*)

A. You're free to make a "way of life" decision instead
of one dictated by necessity. If you've had enough of your

business, why not sell it and keep the real estate? Find a buyer who would rent the property from you—that way, as a landlord, you'd be entitled to keep your present tax deductions against your investment income. You then might give thought to reinvesting in more property in the growth area where you live. It's a one-way property market in growth areas.

Q. I am glad to see that you mentioned apartment buildings as a good investment, but people can't live "rent free" through such ownership. If an owner chooses to live in his building, he should pay rent like everyone else, if for no other reason than to keep the occupancy percentage up where he wants it when he offers the building for sale or trade in the future.

We have owned a 22-unit apartment building on Milwaukee's east side for the last three years, and are going to show at least a 20 percent return. Are there any stocks I could buy, or any other investment I could make, that would net me the same cash return?

Mrs. A. B. F. (Eagle River, Wisconsin)

A. Glad to have your correction. In money terms, you are absolutely right. There's no way to get out of paying rent, whether it's paid in cash or tied up in capital not earning income. The answer to your question is no.

Q. I am 62 and my husband is 59. He is a veteran with a 60 percent disability, for which he receives $151 a month. He earns $8,000 a year. I receive Social Security of $87 a month, and we also have $2,000 in savings. Last year, we put almost $6,000 in a growth fund and also bought *a four-unit apartment building with a 6 percent, 25-year mortgage. We live in one unit and rent the other three, but the rents do not quite cover the cost of mortgage payments and upkeep. We wonder if our investments were wise.*

Mrs. W. O. R. (Cincinnati, Ohio)

A. Don't blame your building if the rent from three-quarters of it doesn't quite cover its carrying costs. Calculate on the basis of whether it would show a profit if the fourth unit were a rent producer, too. By this test, your building investment looks pretty good. I wish I could say the same about your growth fund. Your primary need is income, and a growth fund is a luxury you can't afford. You'll probably do better to keep the building, sell the fund, and shoot for the going rate on savings.

Q. I would like to start an investment program for a daughter who will be entering college in 1972. Most of my current worth is invested in real estate—an apartment building, a business building, and a residence—although I do have small stock holdings and am interested in the stock market. What type of investment would you suggest for my purpose?

Mr. R. E. C. (Morris, Illinois)

A. Your clean, strong, and liquid situation has earned you the right to give advice, not ask for it.

Your summary suggests that you have a feel for direct investment in property. I suspect that you may do better with it—especially if you stick to areas where you have a feel for property values—than if you start dabbling with stocks. Collecting rents is a safe and steady way to stay ahead of tuition bills.

Q. My husband died last August, and I'm trying to sell his business, which is in debt. I have two apartment buildings, one seven years old worth approximately $40,000 (paid for), and another 40 years old and in need of repair ($13,000 balance on mortgage). My primary concern is security and income.

Mrs. F. G. H. (Western Springs, Illinois)

A. From your description you will do well to sell your late husband's business fast, with a minimum of haggling. As to your real estate, it is uneconomic to own a property only seven years old, with no mortgage. It is just as uneconomic to own another 40 years old and in need of repair. I suggest that you put a mortgage on your newer building and use the money to bring your older one into good working order.

Q. We own our home and also a vacant residential lot next door, which is worth about $10,000. We are considering building another house on this lot for about $35,000 and renting it at about $300 a month. Our thinking has been influenced by your expressed preference now for owning real property as opposed to stocks. Do you think our plan is prudent?

Mr. J. P. K. (Northbrook, Illinois)

A I don't think that your idea represents a practical way of putting my general proposition to work. The cost of money and construction is directing investment incentives into the market for existing property, not new building.

Assuming (as I wouldn't) that you can stick to a $35,000 building budget, if you could get a mortgage based on 80 percent of your investment of $45,000 (which I also doubt), you would be tying up $9,000. If you paid only 7 percent interest (doubtful, too), your carrying cost would be $2,520. At only 4 percent, the interest you would be losing on the $9,000 you had tied up in this venture would be another $360. In fact, at present interest rates you would be losing twice as much. Taxes, maintenance, and miscellaneous expenses could easily run another $1,600 or $1,700 a year. Altogether, if everything went right, you would be out over $4,500 annually, and earning only $3,600 in rent.

With your cash reserve, you can afford to sit on your vacant lot until the market comes to you. When it does, you will have a free ride on your customer's money.

Q. I am 30, married, with one child, and we rent our home. My take-home pay as an electronic technician is $245 biweekly. We have $2,000 in savings and loan savings and about $300 in a no-load mutual fund. For the near future, should I: (a) put more money into the mutual fund; (b) put more into the S & L account; (c) take everything out and use it toward a down payment on a three-flat building near us, and borrow the remainder of the down payment from the credit union at work; (d) go to college for an engineering degree, or go into real estate, which perhaps holds a better future?

Mr. N. J. (Oak Park, Illinois)

A. (c) is your best bet for putting your money to work for you once you have accumulated enough savings to leave you a sound cash reserve—$2,000 is altogether too little. (d) is an even better bet for putting yourself to work. But why choose between engineering and real estate? Play for the best of both worlds.

Q. *I was born in Germany more than 68 years ago and have lived through two bad inflations. The first one I was able to meet very well. At the time of the second I was already a United States citizen living here. The money reform of 1948 cost me a large fortune. I received compensation of from 10 to 100 percent for my private assets, but I had to sue the German government eight times to get it. My goal now is to preserve the assets I have left, and I am worried about our creeping inflation that has been gaining momentum during the last two years.*

At my age, there is no point in buying growth stocks. Nobody can guarantee growth of 99 percent of these companies in times like this, anyway. I think land ownership is the best hedge against inflation; then comes commercial property where land constitutes most of the valuation, and next, solid stocks. Would you agree?

Mr. W. H. (Peoria, Illinois)

A. Land ownership is the most reliable way to invest in long-term growth, no matter whether inflation, deflation, or stability is the order of the day. More capital has been accumulated through direct investment in land in this country than through playing with paper. During the inflationary 1950s in Europe, land values appreciated while stock markets broke; and land values are more than ever on the rise there.

But your own experience of the great German inflation that followed World War I should remind you that the most profitable way to play inflation is to owe money—that's the way German big business beat the game when the mark collapsed. They borrowed good dollars first and paid off in cigar store coupons afterward.

Inflation-hedge borrowers need to be sure that their borrowings are long-term, and not subject to call during the money squeeze which invariably accompanies break-away inflation. The best way to borrow at long term is on income-producing property, not on land. Mortgage-lending institutions are normally not permitted to make loans on unimproved land.

Q. In a recent column you mentioned property requiring no labor cost to maintain it as a defense against devaluation. What kind of property falls in this category?

Mrs. J. A. M. (Chicago, Illinois)

A. Land.

Q. I am 66, semi-retired, but keeping active in real estate buying for cash and selling on installment. My net assets—mostly in cash, real estate, and receivables—amount to about $425,000. I also have a $100,000 line of credit at the bank. Should I use this credit to purchase more real estate, or continue buying for cash?

Mr. D. P. S. (Pittsburgh, Pennsylvania)

A. By all means minimize the cash you pay for property, especially at a time when the credit squeeze has enabled buyers to take over large and larger properties by putting up less and less hard cash. Instead, pay with paper, but with paper backed by the assets you are buying, not with your own personal credit. Don't confuse the bank money you have lined up with the mortgage money you can raise by mortgaging improved property.

Q. *Land in our area is an attractive investment, but it doesn't have the liquidity of stocks. How would you suggest we balance our assets?*

Mr. C. R. W. (*Coeur d'Alene, Idaho*)

A. Land is indeed less liquid than stocks, but it offers more long-term gain potential. Land and mutual funds make for good balance, so do land and medium-term bonds of top quality.

Q. *I am a 50-year-old widower with two more children to put through college. My annual income is around $11,500. I own a mortgage-free home and have no debts. Shall I use some of my savings to invest in land in this small-town area?*

Mr. M. J. E. (*Grand Island, Nebraska*)

A. The very best use you can make of your money is to checkerboard small parcels of land in your home town where you are familiar with values. Don't hesitate to use your cash as bait to get local savings institutions to give you mortgages. Small towns are where mortgage money is still to be had—and on reasonable terms. That's the most profitable way to invest in real estate. Take local bank appraisals as a double check on your own judgment of property values.

Q. I have been buying tracts of pine timberlands surrounded by United States Forest Service lands, so that the Government maintains a 24-hour watch over my property, free of charge. This land should be a good inflation hedge. Do you agree?

Mr. W. P. C. (Presho, South Dakota)

A. I agree. You've got it made. You are getting more benefits from the Government than any other taxpayer.

Q. I have an opportunity to invest $10,000 in some good land in Alaska. There is a good chance of oil being on it, as some very successful drilling already is being done nearby. I have $5,000 on hand in a S & L at 5¼ percent. Should I use this amount and borrow the other $5,000 at 6½ percent, or should I keep my $5,000 in reserve and borrow the whole $10,000?

Mr. F. E. N. (Aurora, Illinois)

A. The kind of speculation you describe is no proper use for borrowed money.

Q. My husband and I are farmers, in our forties. We now work 280 acres, of which we own 80 acres. We have about $90,000 to invest and are wondering about buying another 165 acres—which means we would have to go in *debt for about $34,000. Would there be some better low-risk way to invest the money under today's conditions?*

Mrs. G. C. (Standish, Michigan)

A. There is no lower-risk investment for people who know how to work their own land than buying more of it. Modern farming methods make big deals easier to handle than small ones. By all means buy the larger farm—just make sure that the mortgage you get is long-term and non-callable.

Q. *My father and mother, who are both 65, are going to sell their farming business. They are inclined to leave most of the money in a land contract. They believe that taking too much in cash will be foolish because of taxes.*

I am worried that inflation will take most of their interest money and that they will not have enough to live on. This is their only savings, and some advice from you might help them hang onto it. Both have good business sense and will appreciate your answer.

Mrs. T. L. (Detroit, Michigan)

A. I agree with you that your parents have good business sense. In fact, I think that their inclination to keep their money in a land contract is more practical than your more theoretical worry. They are being practical, too, in their calculation that an installment sale—which I suppose is what they have in mind—would defer their tax liability.

Q. *A farm I own produces annually about 12 percent. However, the tenant operator gets half, and the expenses against my half are about 3.8 percent, which leaves 2.2*

percent profit for me. Since land prices are very good now,
I plan to sell. Do you think this is a wise move?

Mrs. D. J. B. (Peoria, Illinois)

A. You are right to sell—even though land prices are
going up. The 2.2 percent net return for an absentee
owner is uneconomically low. But you will probably get
a better price if you take back a mortgage instead of making an all-cash deal. The rising price trend of productive
farmland will protect you if your buyer goes bad on the
mortgage. Purchase-money mortgages taken back by
property sellers are entitled to high rates of return.

Q. The case you make for property investment sounds
great—almost too good to be true. Can anything go wrong?

Miss S. H. (New York City, New York)

A. You are right to ask. If Washington's inflation
fighters continue to fan the flames they claim to have been
putting out, the mid-1970s will bring on the danger of a
serious collision in the mortgage market. Hundreds of
millions of dollars of low-cost, "slow-pay" mortgages were
written early on in the postwar boom—mostly with payment schedules calling for big "balloon" payments
(greater than the actual rate of pay-down) at maturity.
These maturities will fall due mainly on entrepreneur-
owned apartment house developments—hence involving
much larger sums than single-family homes. The mid-
1970s will therefore generate a "once in a generation"
jump of spectacular proportions in the country's need for
new mortgage money in big lots to refinance older properties enjoying higher replacement values, thanks to the

inflation in building and labor costs and property values. This means that the property market could be left vulnerable to a payments crisis if present policies and conditions persist.

The practical way to avoid being caught in any such mortgage refinancing crisis is to make sure that any property investment buys mortgage protection at least 10 years ahead. This is still not hard to find.

CHAPTER V

Mutual Funds

THE mutual funds industry has grown to dominate the stock market by pooling the savings of millions of investors into huge blocks of buying—and selling—power. Their role in the market place reached a peak during the great bull market boom of the middle 1960s, when the cult of growth and performance temporarily overrode the forces of contraction and liquidation generated by the Vietnam-induced inflation and liquidity squeeze.

The fund movement originally got started as a vehicle for providing small investors with the advantages enjoyed by big investors. The first of these advantages is continuing professional money management. Moreover, by amalgamating the savings of many small investors into large units, mutual funds can give the small investor the insurance against risk which comes from diversification. Professional management, risk reduction, and the investment mobility enjoyed only by large pools of money remain the three basic justifications for mutual funds as investments.

But, during the years when the "money game" was the biggest game in the small town known as Wall Street, managers and investors alike became intoxicated with "performance" as the weekly, even the daily, goal. In far too many funds, prudence went out the window and some —but by no means all—major institutional investors, with the life savings of millions of people and their own professional standing as their responsibility, became out-and-out speculators. If the second duty of money management is to increase capital, the first duty is to preserve it. The lesson was relearned the hard way during the long and grinding market slide of 1969-1970.

The irresponsibility of some "growth fund" managers came near to tarring the whole industry. But throughout the excesses of speculative fever and hangover, the minority of sound and prudent managements continued to provide investors with the services for which they were paying.

The industry is itself a highly diversified one with a wide variety of differing investment vehicles. Funds can be classified by objective, such as "growth" or "income." They can be classified by investment media, such as "specialty" funds, which concentrate on chosen industries (like chemicals, or aircraft, or energy, or insurance), or "balanced" funds, which invest in bonds as well as stocks. A new type of fund is directed at the advantages to be gained from investing in real estate. There are "closed-end" funds, the shares of which are limited: to buy them you must make a bid for shares from a present owner. "Open-end" funds issue new shares on demand at a price set by the value of the assets owned by the fund. There is also a distinction between "load" and "no-load" funds: the former take the sales charge in one piece when the shares are bought; the latter have no sales charge.

The sound approach to investing in mutual funds is for the long pull. Different kinds of funds are appropriate for investors with different requirements. No matter what the type of fund chosen, playing it for short-run speculative gain is the way to earn frustration and disappointment. For investors with a long view, mutual funds offer a prudent and proved means of transforming the surplus left from current income into a meaningful stock of capital.

Q. My wife and I have accumulated about $47,000 in assets during our 18 years of marriage, including $10,000 in two mutual funds and $4,000 in common stocks. We are interested in growth-type common stocks that we could invest in and just put away for 15 to 20 years and forget about. Is this feasible, or is it wise to keep watching and switching to more attractive issues?

Mr. J. W. E. (Portland, Oregon)

A. If your strategy is to put equities away on a 15-to-20-year time scale, you will probably do better with mutual funds than switching in and out of stocks which come and go with fashions in growth. If you are committing yourself to mutual funds for the long pull, play for the long pull and don't judge performance by flash quotes.

Q. I am 27, single, with $1,000 to invest. I carry $2,000 life insurance, and can save $100 a month. Mutual funds have been recommended. What do you advise? And should I invest a certain amount and leave it, or add to my investment regularly?

Miss N. B. (Grand Rapids, Michigan)

A. Good for you! Follow a regular plan. You are young enough to play for the long term. Deposit your savings into your passbook account; and, after you receive each quarter's interest, withdraw a regular amount and switch it into a growth fund. Do it each quarter, without regard to whether the stock market is in or out of favor at the time. But don't get caught over-invested and with too little cash reserve for any emergency.

Q. *About a year ago I wrote you that I was planning to divide $15,000 among 26 common stocks. You replied that my list was too long and that I was stacking the averages against myself. Recently I read a study which assumed an equal initial investment in each of 1,856 New York Stock Exchange common stocks, and which showed that in the period from 1945 through 1965 there was no 10-year period in which the hypothetical investor earned less than 11 percent a year. A random selection of stocks gave approximately the same results. I now propose to invest my $15,000 in $5,000 and $2,000 amounts in four mutual funds. Would you recommend this?*

Col. J. C. D. (Park Forest, Illinois)

A. Absolutely. A professional military man like you will agree that no two wars are won in the same way. Investment history doesn't repeat itself, either. The years 1945 through 1965 saw the entire breadth of the market participate with the economy in its unprecedented profitable expansion. In those years it was harder to pick losers than winners.

After 1965, the market became steadily more selective. Before it floundered, as it did, the odds rose against any bet on a single stock paying off. This explained the growing disposition of market professionals with good records to sit tight and let the froth settle. All any investor needs is one winner at a time. But the professionals can let their winners make money for them, while the amateurs need their winners just to make up for their losses.

Q. I am an engineer, 29 years old, with a 4-year-old son who I anticipate will be going to college 13 or 14 years from now. I would like to start some form of investment program now, in order to provide funds for his education. Could you please recommend the "best" (that is, providing safety with reasonable appreciation) form of investment with this goal in mind?

Mr. R. M. S. (Naperville, Illinois)

A. Mutual funds are the answer to your problem; and the solution of problems such as yours is the most economic and, also, the most socially constructive service mutual funds render.

The Investment Company Act of 1940, policed by the SEC, requires all fund salesmen to give their sales prospects an opportunity to scrutinize more than one fund in order to determine which is appropriate for their investment purpose, and incidentally, to put the potential investor on notice that there is no such thing as standard mutual fund merchandise.

Q. Will you please explain to me what the Keogh plan is?

Mr. J. C. (Palatine, Illinois)

A. Sponsored by former Congressman Eugene Keogh, it grants to professional people and self-employed the right to set aside 10 percent of their income or $2,500 a year, whichever is less, to go into a fund, the investment proceeds of which are tax-free until withdrawn at retirement. The funds can be set up through banks, insurance companies, or mutual funds.

Q. *Are mutual funds a good buy? I am 60, retired, and have shares in several funds set up under deed of trust for my family. We have no debts, own our home, and I have $100,000 life insurance. My wife is 45, and we have two sons, 20 and 15. We have $218,000 in short-term Governments yielding 5½ percent, and we need $20,000 a year from our investments. I am considering two more funds.*

Dr. J. H. E. (Dayton, Ohio)

A. You certainly own enough funds to be able to figure out the answer for yourself. From looking at your list, I suspect that you're the kind of prospect fund salesmen dream about, although I can't tell whether you're buying them blind or whether you are discriminating enough to be using different vehicles for different purposes in order to diversify your objectives and hedge your bets.

Mutual funds are as good as their managements. Some of them have become high-risk ways to play the market, and it can't be said loud enough or often enough that this is not what mutual funds are for. If you want to add to your list, I'd recommend that you pick one of the more conservative, old established major funds. Some of the best funds came out of the Depression decade bigger and in better shape than they were in at the onset.

The conservative funds are relatively easy to distinguish from the speculative performance funds which were all the rage when the stock market seemed a one-way affair. They looked like stick-in-the-muds in 1967. The conservative funds' portfolio holdings are concentrated in the securities of groups that have been leaders in their fields for some years. They do not turn their portfolios over on the theory that they can out-trade the market and have remained investment funds instead of being seduced by the lure of speculation. The importance of making the distinction is a reminder not to buy any fund without first looking at the portfolio to make sure that you understand what the investment job of the fund is. The salesman, by the way, is obligated to tell you.

Q. I am a complete novice at stock investments, and I know that you will say I need the guidance of a competent broker. But first I would appreciate your opinion, because I know you would not be biased.

I am 61 years old. My assets consist of a paid-up $10,000 endowment policy maturing at age 65, and something over $25,000 invested in three mutual funds—one balanced fund and two growth funds. Also, I expect a sale of real property to net me about $40,000, which I'm tempted to put into my growth funds. What would you advise?

Mr. H. D. (Skokie, Illinois)

A. I appreciate your confidence in my objectivity. Today's complications are so novel that even old pros who pride themselves on their wealth of experience will do well to share your humble pie. Change, when it is big enough, makes novices of us all.

We are in the first inflation since World War I rapid enough and sustained enough to have produced higher interest rates. In fact, the cost of money has been rising faster than commodity prices. Professionals in the yield game now have an opportunity to latch onto high yields that will net substantial gains during the next period of low interest rates. Consequently, a great deal of professional investment money that had been primarily growth-minded is now being rerouted into investment for income. Fund investment is long-pull investment, and the investments which balanced funds are making now in safe high yields will show big gains for the long pull. The growth funds have had their day, and the balanced funds are having theirs. It promises to last longer.

Q. My husband is a clergyman, and his salary has never been high. We have put three children through college. Our resources are meager: adequate health insurance, a life and accident policy, $3,000 in savings, and a pension plan that will pay only about $100 a month. With retirement getting close, we are thinking of taking $2,000 from our savings and investing it either in mutual funds or in some growth stocks. Would you advise doing either? We will probably have about $1,000 a year for the next few years to invest.

Mrs. G. B. (Chicago, Illinois)

A. A mutual fund would suit your circumstances. But you will do better to think in terms of a balanced fund at the moment than a growth fund. Be sure that the balanced fund you buy is run by a management that also operates a growth fund so that, when risks are reduced foɪ small investors, you can switch to a growth fund without a cost penalty.

Q. I disagree with your recent advice to invest $10,000 from the sale of a home in a mutual fund instead of in 5 percent savings certificates. The $10,000 will purchase only $9,200 in market value of securities.

Income might net $460 a year after deducting management fees, and tax obligations would accrue on dividends and capital gains. But $10,000 invested in 5 percent savings certificates would return $500 a year without cost of any kind and not subject to market depreciation.

Mr. A. H. F. (Fort Lauderdale, Florida)

A. Dissent and debate are the tools of decision-making. I appreciate your helpful counter-arguments. Herewith rebuttals.

Your complaint seems to be directed against the purchase of all load funds, at any time. But the "load" paid in sales charges buys professional management: if the return which professional management earns for the amateur investor *over a period of time* doesn't more than pay for the sales charges, the answer is to buy better management. The boom-and-slump market of recent years has provided investors with the opportunity of judging competitive track records in good times and bad. By the way, you'll do well to remember that the interest earned on savings certificates does bear a cost, too—the cost of tax payments at ordinary income rates. Year in and year out, any professional management worth its keep can accrue a higher net return on capital than the after-tax return on savings certificates—that's the difference between savings and investment, about which you are confused.

I have never advocated mutual fund investment as a way of beating the market on fast turns or for people who don't have time and patience for the long pull. The younger and more amateurish the investor, the better suited funds are for keeping what's in the basket protected while getting it carried.

Q. I am just now 58 years old and my children are married. My wife and I are wondering about the best type of investment for the future. I expect to work at least 10 to 15 years more, which is altogether possible in my profession.

I understand there are certain mutual funds that do not charge a percentage for their services. Would you recommend this type of investment? We are interested in growth.

Rev. P. V. (Cincinnati, Ohio)

A. "No-load" funds make no sales charge. They do pay management fees themselves, but do not pass the cost directly on to the customer. Instead, a cash charge is made on the assets of the fund.

But it's the past record of a fund you should look at when considering it as an investment. Whether it is a "load" or a "no-load" fund it is performance that matters. A "no-load" fund that loses half your capital is more expensive than a "load" fund that charges you up to 8 percent on the way in, makes it back for you in a reasonable period of time—measured in years, not weeks—and conserves your capital instead of dissipating it. Don't generalize about either "load" or "no-load" funds; as Al Smith used to say, "Look at the record."

One charge you should watch out for, however, is a performance fee which some funds take out as an incentive for their managers. Private advisors try to play this game, too, but don't you get involved in it. Such incentives led in 1967-1968 to serious abuses of sound investment practice in pursuit of day-to-day performance.

Q. Two questions: (1) Should the possibility of a substantial drop in stock prices affect an established program of monthly investments in a mutual fund? (2) Why is the sales commission of load funds so high? It seems to me that I am paying a lot of money to the wrong people.

Mr. V. W. (Chicago, Illinois)

A. The answer to your first question is no. The great value of monthly investment programming is that the programmer ends up averaging out the peaks and valleys of short- and intermediate-term fluctuations. These programs are for long-term accumulation. Anyone starting them should put the temptation to beat short-term market swings behind him.

The answer to your second question reflects the high cost of doing the sales job which has opened up a mass market to fund managements and has enabled the small investor to realize advantages heretofore restricted to larger investors—notably diversification and access to professional management.

Actually, the sales load falls sharply as the size of the investment rises. Many small investors who try to outdo fund management performance on their own by trading the market wind up with higher costs in stock exchange commissions—let alone losses—than if they had simply absorbed a fund sales load on the way in (which also entitles the investors to get out gratis).

Q. I am 76 and depend for more than 50 percent of my living expenses on income from investments. I started investing in 1954 after my husband's death and have stuck mainly to mutual funds for diversification. I enclose a list of my holdings. My objectives are (1) safety of principal; (2) income; and (3) growth—in that order. It seems to me that a gain of about $1,700 on an investment of $65,000 is very slight over a 12-year period. I am sure I need a good investment counselor, but don't know how to find one.

Mrs. M. F. B. (Chicago, Illinois)

A. Your theories have been sound. Only your practice has been punk. A $65,000 investment portfolio that has managed a gain of only $1,700 over 12 years of the biggest bull market in history is a prime candidate for liquidation. You say that one of your main objectives is income, compatible with safety of principal. But you have invested nearly half your equity in a poor-performing open-end fund, and a like amount in five closed-end funds. All investment companies (closed- or open-end) fluctuate with the market; and all closed-end investment companies pay low incomes. Consequently, you have exposed yourself to the risk of market fluctuation, but you have not been buying yourself an income high enough to warrant the risk—or, in fact, a high income.

Q. I take issue with your statement that "closed-end investment companies pay low incomes." It seems to me you completely ignored the very handsome capital gains dividends which some keep paying year after year.

Fund Fan (Chicago, Illinois)

A. Closed-end investment companies can indeed be very profitable investments, depending on their management performance, but not because of their high yields. There is a fundamental difference between regular dividend income flow and nonrecurrent payouts from gains when and as taken—that's why the Securities and Exchange Commission and the Internal Revenue Service agree that all dividends must be designated as one or the other. Open-end investment funds pay capital gains dividends, too.

Q. The company I work for is withdrawing from business, and I am eligible, at 56, for retirement benefits. I will work at another job at least until age 65. The retirement benefits, if taken now, would amount to $76 a month for life; or if not taken until age 65, to $146 a month. I feel I should take the $76 a month now and invest it in some mutual fund. Do you agree?

Mr. A. P. G. (Westchester, Illinois)

A. I do. A mutual fund should be able to produce more for you over the next nine-year swing than your retirement fund is committed to do. Inasmuch as you will have a fixed dollar amount to invest each month, you will do well to inquire about the advantages of dollar averaging.

Q. I am a 15-year-old boy. I deliver the Detroit Free Press and earn about $8 a week. I would like to invest my earnings, but don't know where.

Won't you please tell me what to do? I want to get into a planned program that will take me through the next 20 years starting now.

Mr. M. R. B. (Mount Clemens, Michigan)

A. More power to you. Hope I'm around 20 years from now to ask your advice.

Tell one of the local investment dealers to pick out a conservative no-load fund for you. Put a fixed amount into it every three months. If you have any trouble finding a no-load fund, write back to me. The reason a no-load fund makes sense for you is that you have so little to get started with.

Q. You recently answered a letter from a newsboy and recommended a no-load mutual fund. I'm a newsboy, too. Would you please give me the names and addresses of some of these funds?

Mr. W. S. (Wayne, Michigan)

A. Look in your daily newspaper for the tabulation of mutual funds. The no-load funds are the ones whose daily bid and asked prices are always the same.

Q. We have $20,000 to be used for college expenses for our three sons from 1970 through 1977. To combat inflation, and possibly increase the total, we plan to invest $10,000 of this in a no-load fund. Do you consider this wise?

Mr. H. B. (Beloit, Wisconsin)

A. Funds will help you help your sons, but I question your judgment in limiting your choice to no-load funds. It can't be said often enough that the test is performance for you, not profit to the fund management. Your only hope of doing well with any fund investment depends on the ability of the fund management to make money for itself by managing your money well.

Q. *I am retired, with Social Security and pension income which is not as much as I would like. I have $135,000 in stocks and a mutual fund, $14,000 in 6 percent bonds, $5,000 in cash, $3,000 in E-bonds and $4,000 in Treasury notes. My stocks yield about 4.5 percent, and most have gone down in price. Do you think I have too many common stocks for the size of my holdings?*

Mrs. H. T. (Evanston, Illinois)

A. Sounds to me like you have. You've also lumped a topnotch income fund in with your common stocks which are losers. You would do well to switch some of them into it.

Q. *I purchased shares in a closed-end fund for the long pull. I'm happy with my investment, but this fund is selling at 20 to 25 percent below net asset value. Can you explain why?*

Mr. H. A. (Lake Bluff, Illinois)

A. Closed-end funds generally sell at discounts under their net asset value—as open-end mutual funds by law can't do. The reason is simply that buyers aren't willing to bid more for these stocks. The time to buy a closed-end fund is when you know it is about to be liquidated. Any time one is, the discount under asset value turns into capital gain for the buyer.

Even though you're happy with your investment, your reasoning reflects confusion. The time to buy a leverage fund is when you think its particular investments are likely to do best—not at random for the long pull.

Q. You have lately advised investing in apartments and income-producing property, but that means $50,000 or more. What do you recommend for us small investors? I now have about $3,000 in two growth funds. I would like to invest $1,000 more.

Mr. D. E. O. (Clarkston, Washington)

A. You are confusing horses with apples. Real estate investment is primarily for income. Investment in growth stocks takes you to the opposite end of the money-using spectrum, for it puts the emphasis on future gain, explicitly sacrificing income in the present.

With your limited cash, I suggest you will do better to keep your thousand dollars in a savings account.

I would also advise you to contact the sponsors of your two growth funds with a view to switching them into the income funds each of these managements also runs. Fund managements sponsoring more than one fund permit their shareholders the privilege of switching from one of their funds to another without additional commission charges.

Q. I am a dentist, 59 years old. We own everything free and clear—our home, clinic building, and 30 acres of Florida citrus acreage which is worth more than double its cost 15 years ago. It has averaged a 10 to 15 percent net return.

We also have substantial stockholdings and savings, and I carry $65,000 in life insurance—which leads to my writing you. One $10,000 policy—a $100-a-month retirement income—is about to mature; present cash value is about $17,000. I notice that the payments tend to reduce principal, so that eventually no balance would go to the estate. This goes against my Scottish nature. So we have been thinking of taking the $17,000, adding another $3,000 to it and putting the sum into a $100-a-month "systematic withdrawal" mutual fund plan to help pay our two girls' college expenses. What do you think?

Mr. H. D. K. (Detroit, Michigan)

A. As your experience shows, more money is made investing in property than in speculating on securities. As to your retirement policy, I think your thinking is practical. Are you aware that you can buy insurance and mutual funds in a package? Such a "package" fund may suit your purpose.

Q. I am 35 years of age, married, with three small children. I own a retail office equipment store that I purchased in 1961 for $60,000 with $3,000 down. I have since reduced the note to $7,500 and will retire it soon. My net assets in the business are $85,000.

I also own a 40 percent interest in a small motel on ocean-front property and a $30,000 home with a $23,000 mortgage. My average income is $25,000 a year. I keep about $20,000 in my business account, and have $20,000 in savings accounts and savings certificates. I have estab-

lished trust accounts for my wife and children, and have sufficient insurance.

I now believe I can save $5,000 a year, and I am thinking of investing in a no-load mutual fund, perhaps starting with an initial purchase of $15,000 from my cash and adding to it at the rate of $400 a month. What would you advise?

Mr. B. E. J. (Orlando, Florida)

A. You have done so outstandingly well that I think you owe it to yourself to see if you can't figure out how to handle your own affairs better than a fund could. Funds are mainly for people who lack your impressive business skill, or who have reached a time of life at which they don't want to be bothered trying, or who haven't enough cash to make direct investment meaningful. But you have accumulated capital for yourself at a faster rate than any fund would or could. Also, you are well enough fixed and your family obligations are well enough protected that you can afford to do a bit of long-shot speculating. Why don't you give thought to going it alone, with a view to building your own fund?

Q. Over and above all the regulations we read about, how can the average, mature small-town investor, who has heard so many lurid stories about security sales malpractices, be on guard against being taken by greedy mutual fund salesmen?

Mrs. M. J. (Redhook, Iowa)

A. The worst single security sales abuse, which no regulation can reach, is the practice called "churning."

This describes what salesmen do to chalk up commissions at the expense of their customers' capital.

Once a fund buyer has paid the load charge, the very worst thing that can happen to him is to be fast-talked into liquidating the holding and being switched into another load fund, absorbing another sales load charge. Unscrupulous salesmen have been known to clip customers in this way more than twice in one year.

The SEC has been able to reach and to regulate the companion practice of churning portfolios at the management level as a safeguard to fund-holders against netting inordinate brokerage fees.

CHAPTER VI

Stocks — Principles

THE American stock market is as widely misunderstood as the motives of Presidents—and that's going some. The great popular illusion assumes that stock prices rise and fall with speedups and slowdowns in business conditions. Wall Street's demoralization in the first half of 1970 constitutes the latest proof that this is not so. For if it were, the stock market would merely have been dipping. Instead, it went on a toboggan ride. This points to maladies deeper-seated than those registered by the standard economic indicators.

Once the idea sinks in that the primary influence on the stock market is financial and political, not—believe it or not!—economic, the causes of the debacle in Wall Street become more comprehensible, and so do their consequences.

Everyone knows about the constitutional system of checks and balances responsible for the dual sovereignty over money in which Congress participates as an equal partner with the President and his appointees. The financial consequences of this system expose the securities markets to the hazards of getting caught in the middle of a political no-man's land any time the President and the Congress have a falling out. For if the special area of Presidential sovereignty is concentrated in the war-making powers, the special area of Congressional sovereignty is concentrated in money-voting powers.

When the President and Congress fight, the weapon Congress uses is the money power; and, whether it wins or loses, the securities markets, which depend upon a free flow of easy money, cannot avoid being hurt. The necessary condition for a strong stock market is an atmosphere of political cooperation between the President and Congress.

A President on bad terms with Congress can hope to manage only if he can borrow less, rather than more. But when the President and Congress get involved in fisticuffs over money, and when the President and his appointees are obliged to borrow not merely more, but more than they themselves dare try or are able to keep track of, the resultant turbulence in the political atmosphere spreads turbulence into the money markets. It was this politically induced turbulence in the money markets that in turn rocked, shook, and tore apart the structure of the stock market in 1969 and 1970.

Wall Street is more full of old rules than a standard compendium of old wives' tales. The oldest rule in the professional book is that, at any given time, the next move the market makes is the move that the technical pressures —the supply and demand for stocks—prompt it to make. In the short run, the market rises and falls in response to the constant seesawing between the pressures of buyers and those of sellers. It is only in the long run that the

fundamental political and financial pressures assert
enough external pressure on the market to change its
direction.

A divergence between the dominant technical pressures
of the moment and the long-term underlying fundamental pressures is normal. This is what makes the stock
market such a tricky track to run on. Again and again,
solemn, earnest, and simple-minded students of the fundamentals are thrown off balance by the spectacle of the
market "going in the wrong direction"—their way of saying that it is bucking the fundamental pressures. But it
almost always does when the technical pressures argue
against the fundamentals.

The volume-price ratio is the place to look for the technical story. This sounds more formidable than it really is.
All it means is that the market can make its moves up
or down in one of two ways, on a big volume of transactions or on a small volume. A price move on big volume
can be taken as authoritative and impressive, if sustained,
while price moves on small volume are suspect.

The story of the fundamentals is written into the relationship between dividends and yields, and another jar-
gonny but basically simple term describes this relationship.
The "yield spread" defines the relationship between the
yield on investment in stocks—dividend divided by price
—and the interest rate earned by investing in bonds. When
the way ahead is clear for the stock market, there is a
positive yield spread, which means that the dividends
paid by stocks are yielding a higher rate of return than
the interest to be had from bonds. This definition of a
positive yield spread—which is good for stocks—does
double duty in defining a negative yield spread: when

bonds pay higher rates than stocks yield in dividends.

A strong stock market can hold its own for a while against a reasonably small negative yield spread, but the rule of thumb is that a negative yield spread of 2 percent or more, if sustained over a period of months, is guaranteed first to stop the stock market in its tracks and then to send it spinning. It happened back in 1929 when the market went merrily on its way ignoring the runaway in interest rates that was tolling the bell for its future.

After World War II, the great bull market not only took in its stride recessionary intervals, which brought interest rates down, but also survived a long seige of money costing more than stocks paid in dividends.

When it was starting up, dividend yields on stocks did not have to be very high to seem generous. The pace of inflation was quickening fast enough to be controversial during the late 1940s and early 1950s, but the price commanded by money was then still literally next to nothing. Dividends were free to increase, and, in fact, they did while interest rates were not a problem—the positive yield spread was widening.

The next phase in the history of the bull market—its movement from maturity toward disintegration—can be written in terms of the psychological switch on the part of investors from yield to growth and the simultaneous narrowing, and eventual disappearance, of a positive yield spread.

While the stock-minded public progressively subordinated its original interest in dividend income to the hope of buying future growth, the money markets were delivering a long-drawn-out, slow-motion punch to the stock market. By the time stockholders were jolted out of their intoxicated infatuation with growth, money rented out to borrowers was earning more than twice as much as money invested in stocks.

While the bull market was still on, the cult of equity, and the presumption that too much money was chasing too few stocks, promised to make obsolete the older rule relating stock prices to interest rates.

All the drum-beating about the premium price each dollar of earnings could be expected to command in the stock market blurred the realization that stock prices pegged to earnings hang on nothing more firm than a hope and a promise. Reduced to their hard-rock-bottom investment value, earnings themselves represent essentially a market in futures.

When market analysts speak of the prices of stocks capitalizing each dollar of earnings at a given rate—whether 5 times earnings or 50 times earnings—they are really using shorthand. What investors want to do is look behind that dollar of present earnings to the future dollar of dividends they can anticipate. The question to ask about earnings is whether they can be translated into hard-cash dividends.

This calculation remains in force even when investors are excited by speculative fever and make a point of expressing their disdain for mere income, cutting capers instead about their preference for capital gains. Also investors buying growth today and for the immediate future will sooner or later reach the time of life when income is what matters. The need to make the transition from earnings growth to cash dividend receipts also applies to fiduciaries obligated to deliver cash payouts on schedule to beneficiaries. An interesting sidelight on this point comes from Edson Gould, whom I regard as the most talented stock market technician in Wall Street. He calculates that from 1900 to 1970 the secular up-trend in stock prices (1,359 percent) has been supported dollar for dollar by the increase in dividend payouts (1,336 percent).

Now the question about dividends is tied up in the argument about the money squeeze. The rising cost of money suggests the severity of the 1970 bear market problem of paying dividends. But more serious than the actual cost of money to corporate borrowers has been the rapid rate of run-down in corporate liquidity, as well as the drastic shortening in the terms of borrowings and the resultant speed-up in the rate at which corporations are racing to meet maturing debt. The 1970 bear market has brought management up against the moment of truth when dollars earned may have to be cycled back into the repayment of short-term debt and the replacement of working capital no longer financeable by debt.

The market's show of ebullience in 1967-1968 added up to a bet that credit-crunch conditions would not return. The bet was lost. By 1969 the drift in the market recalled Dr. Samuel Johnson's quip in response to criticism of a woman preaching a bad sermon: "Sir, a woman's preaching is like a dog's walking on his hind legs. It is not done well, but you are surprised to find it done at all." By then, it was no longer remarkable that the stock market had been stopped from going up, but rather that it had managed to avoid being knocked down still further.

With 1970 came the new era of fear and insecurity.

Stock-chasers watched the market like a crowd at the circus, buzzing with suspense over whether the performer would scramble to safety or break his neck.

The popular presumption is that any tight-rope walking act is over quickly. But while Wall Street is certainly not above staging a circus from time to time, its dramatic moves never resolve themselves quickly. On the contrary, its tests of strength are protracted, recurrent, and—more often than not—deceptive.

The long-term test that has been facing the market is one that Wall Street terms "distribution." As long as the bull market was on, it was marked by the accumulation of huge blocks of stocks—from I.B.M. through the lowest-grade unmarketable junk—on the part of institutional investors. Consequently, when the public left the stock market, it left the market at the mercy of large block traders and without the support of individual investors.

At the beginning of 1969 and again in 1970, I interviewed Sander Landfield, partner in New York's leading odd-lot firm of Carlisle de Coppet & Co., for another of my *Chicago Tribune* columns. Of all Wall Street's long-standing professional bulls, none had been more right in his judgment of the market than Landfield. But when he spoke to me in 1969, he could see no hope of avoiding a downturn in the stock market until the little fellow came back to it.

"My main concern," he said in our first interview, "is about the market's ability to distribute securities in 1969. It is not that the game has changed, but that the market-makers have.

"Fewer people are controlling more money which is not their own and on which, in many instances, they have leveraged a good deal of borrowing," he explained. "A market in which large numbers of investors directly influence securities prices is much thicker than one influenced primarily by a handful of fund managers. Volume developed directly by individual investors has declined considerably. This eventually can affect the market's liquidity.

"The underlying liquidity of the market is suffering deterioration, and this really is the bothersome aspect of present market conditions. At some point this trend will be manifest to a lot of investors, but there will be little they can do about it because they won't be able to liquidate their positions."

After the preliminary break of 1969 had confirmed the timeliness of Landfield's warning, I asked him in January, 1970, "What will bring the small investor back?" Said Landfield, "Relaxation of inflationary pressure. I suppose this will be brought about when the abnormally tight-money situation finally eases. The big incentive is yield. Once stocks come close to giving yields as rich as bonds, the little fellow will switch back from bonds, which he's buying now, to stocks.

"There's never going to be a perfect relationship between yield on equities as against fixed income, but the investing public would be willing to forgo part of the spread on the assumption that the equity will appreciate.

"Meanwhile, of course, the little man may find that he has less disposable funds to go into any sort of investment. But eventually bargains will bring him back on a direct basis."

Q. I cannot recall a time when you were optimistic about the stock market. Is your objection to the present state of the market, or to the stock market generally for anyone other than a pro?

Mr. L. G. E. (Valparaiso, Indiana)

A. My warnings are aimed strictly and solely at the continuing high-risk condition of the stock market. It has become even more risky for the professionals than for the amateurs: the reason being that the market has been suffering from an acute case of illiquidity, and the professionals are obviously more vulnerable to a crisis of market illiquidity than the amateurs—after all, they are stuck with big blocks, and they chalk up their performance by selling and taking profits when and as they can.

Answering the first part of your question, I was the first writer on finance with a public following to recommend computer, aerospace, and metal stocks for the long pull to the institutional community—back when the settlement of the Korean War was provoking fears of a stock market break. As late as November, 1963, I scored another such first, forecasting that the Dow-Jones Industrial Average would go up to 1,000 by the end of 1966, as it did. I have been bearish since, and it has not reached that high again.

Q. The new bear market seems to have remained as selective as the bull market was in its later phase. What standards would you suggest for concluding that any given stocks may have hit bottom and be ready to form a new investment base?

Mr. E. H. (East Orange, New Jersey)

A. Two. The first to look for is hard-cash investment in net worth which reduces a company's ratio of short-term debt to capital. The second is the sight of the last go-go performance mutual fund dumping the last "performance" stock. The bigger the participation of performance-fund ownership in a stock, the more bearish its prospects under today's reversed rules of the road.

Q. *Would lower interest rates help the stock market?*

Miss E. O. (Salt Lake City, Utah)

A. That's like asking me if I could see better if you stopped poking your finger in my eye.

Q. *What is the difference between an official devaluation of the United States dollar and an official United States increase in the price of gold? In the event of either happening, would United States dollars buy less in the U.S.A.? How should one best protect himself against loss of purchasing power? Are stocks a protection against these events?*

Mr. R. S. (Berwyn, Illinois)

A. An official United States increase in the dollar price of gold would automatically have the effect of devaluing the foreign-exchange value of the dollar. But I doubt that any such Washington move is in the cards—because a by-product of such an action would be to accelerate the domestic American inflation.

The domestic dollar may continue to lose purchasing power anyway. In the first phase of inflation, stocks generally do provide a hedge against inflation. But the worse inflation becomes, the more selective and risky the stock-hedging game gets.

Q. Would you advise short sales of selected issues in anticipation of a projected downward move?

Mr. D. G. A. (Spokane, Washington)

A. Short selling is for professionals—not least because it involves borrowing—so watch your step.

Another way to accomplish the same purpose is to buy puts from the put-and-call brokers who advertise on the financial pages of your newspaper. The owner of a put is entitled literally to "put" a given number of shares of a given stock at a given price, which means that the cost of his put leaves him in the same position as the short seller without his having to go into debt. If the market goes up instead of down, all he is out is the price he pays for the privilege.

Q. I am interested in what may be called "distressed stocks"—those of otherwise sound companies that have fallen into difficulty, or new companies having start-up problems, so that the market quotation on the stock has fallen. I'd like to learn how to identify these companies and how to evaluate them as potential investments. Can you tell me how to satisfy my interest in these stocks?

Mr. C. M. (Kansas City, Missouri)

A. Who wouldn't like to learn how to play this game? It's the most profitable one in town, and it's the one that successful take-over operators play. Watch the companies with the best take-over records, and you'll see that they've been picking up insurance, tobacco, and finance companies. You may be able to spot a trend in the types of companies they find attractive. The depressed stocks of companies with a future always come back for investors with patience.

Q. *Within a year I will retire at 65 and can use additional income. Eleven years ago I purchased 10 shares of blue-chip stock. Since that time, with stock splits and purchase of split shares, my holdings have increased to 104 shares. My initial investment of $5,000 is now $34,000, but my current return on market value of these stocks is only about 1 percent. Is there any way I can switch into securities with higher yields without an immediate payment of capital gains tax?*

Mr. J. R. (Riverside, Illinois)

A. No. The so-called "switch funds" used to be usable for this purpose, but that game has been ended. Of course, you could minimize your immediate tax bite by selling a bit each year. It would certainly be prudent for you to start on such a program right now. If you switch the proceeds into tax-exempts, you will average up your overall yield dramatically. Of course, your present yield on your original investment is nothing to complain about.

Q. *I am 51, and my wife and I have a yearly income of $14,000, not including income from investments. Our $20,000 home is paid for, and we have $4,000 in a mutual fund, $8,000 in discount and real estate investment houses, $4,000 in credit union, $15,000 in insurance, and two cars paid for. We have a surplus of $1,000 about every two months to invest. I have a co-worker who has done tre-*

mendously well in 30 or 40 speculative and nonspecula-
tive stocks, and I sometimes wonder if I should be in there.
Shall I borrow $10,000 on my insurance and put the
money in some investment?

Mr. E. F. D. (Cincinnati, Ohio)

A. You have done a pretty good job of staying ahead
of inflation, but you seem to be listening to a siren song.
If your co-worker is in the same bracket as you, he cannot possibly have done "tremendously well" in 30 or 40
speculative and nonspeculative stocks. He couldn't have
had the capital to spread over that many issues. If he
weren't spoofing you, Wall Street would have caught on
to his secret and hired him away from your joint employer
for a million dollars or more in take-home pay.

Seriously, the odds are that, the more stocks he played
with, the more losers he had. His winners would have
done well merely to pay for his losers. You can afford a
speculative fling—so long as you don't overdo it. But the
worst way to finance it is to borrow on your insurance.
Approach speculation as the financial equivalent of a
vacation: to be paid for with hard cash the loss of which
creates no hardship. If you decide to speculate, I don't
think that you want to commit more than $1,000 a year,
and you can't go very far—or very far wrong—on this.

Q. I expect the market to fall still further. If you agree,
what do you think of taking a short position in a hot elec-
tronics stock using a stop-loss order? I have a few dollars
I could use in a speculative venture.

Mr. J. A. (New York, New York)

A. That is one of the worst things you could do. Stubborn short-selling speculation by amateurs has provided one reason why the bull market lasted as long as it did. Every time the old pros catch a new flock of greedy innocents short, the glamour stocks, which attract the amateur short-selling, are guaranteed another upward move. The odds are still high that the cards are stacked against small players who short the stocks of companies whose names end in "-on" or "-onics."

Q. I am a 25-year-old married man, with one child. I have been out of college for two years and have been able to save some money, which I would like to invest in stocks. Would you help me with the following questions? The more people I ask, the more different answers I get.

1. What industries would you recommend as long-term investments?

2. Should emphasis be given to yield and to price-earnings?

Mr. D. C. A. (Addison, Illinois)

A. 1. American industries assured of steady work and expanding markets regardless of business conditions include: copper, aluminum, uranium, power equipment, pollution control, labor-saving materials handling equipment, and medical and hospital equipment. The qualifications for inclusion in this select circle are the ability to run at capacity despite slumps suffered by customers and the ability to grow faster than gross national product.

2. Certainly emphasis should be given to both price-earnings ratios and yields. In fact, the price-earnings ratio should be calculated as an investment in future yield.

Dividends, to be deemed safe, need to be covered by earnings at a conservative ratio of 2 : 1 (except for utilities, whose guaranteed rates of return entitle them to pay out higher proportions of their earnings as dividends than companies obliged to compete). Normally, the greater the growth factor, the lower the yield. The high-yielding copper stocks are a special case.

CHAPTER VII

Stocks—Particulars

FOR years, everyone has agreed that the Dow-Jones Industrial Average is an imperfect and incomplete measure of market performance. It covers the activity of 30 leading industrial stocks, but they are the big names of a generation ago.

These are the old blue chips, the leading industrial companies, which have grown big and are deemed to be well financed. They include big names like General Foods, General Motors, and American Can, and a proven record for safety provides their attraction for investors. But they are not likely to make them money in the form of capital gains. Talking about the old blue chips means going back to the concept of the positive yield spread—to be worthwhile they need to pay a higher rate in dividends than can be obtained in interest on bonds.

During the last two decades of comfortable growth in American business, economic forecasters and investment analysts fell into the habit of rating the performance of an industry or a company poor if it improved its earnings by only 5 or 10 percent a year. So generously did affluence nurture the stock market that stocks which compounded gains at no more than 10 to 25 percent a year were considered laggards in the growth competition.

Thus, when the growth cult came into its own, Wall Street's professional corps of stock market analysts developed their own special yardstick for measuring the performance of the growth stocks, the new blue chips—I.B.M., Xerox, Polaroid, and the rest of the galaxy. The growth cultists tended to be increasingly individualistic in their choice of junior-grade I.B.M.s, but all of them accepted the same simple principle: any representative index of growth stocks will rise twice as fast as the Dow-Jones index. And there is no doubt about it, the great growth stocks have demonstrated that they are much more volatile than the staid old investment favorites Aunt Jane inherited from grandfather, when a 5 percent dividend return was the criterion of investor acceptance.

With the new blue chips the money-making exercise is aimed at gain, not yield. While the old blue chips produced the staples of yesterday and today, the new ones have been meeting the presumed needs of today and tomorrow.

But the pattern becomes more complex just because business conditions are continually changing. Five years ago, in identifying transportation stocks, General Motors was deemed to be a growth stock of the last generation, and Boeing one of the new. Now anything to do with aerospace has fallen on hard times, while GM qualifies as a "money" stock—as if it were a utility free from the need to issue more shares.

In fact, aerospace stocks, sensitive as they are to the volatile cycle in Washington's willingness and ability to advance money to them, can now be classed with cyclical stocks—stocks that go with the business cycle. Why shouldn't they, in this day when the business cycle swings with the Washington cycle of political finance?

The cyclical group also includes textile, steel, housing, auto and appliance, machinery and machine tool, hotel stocks, etc. All their stops and starts, speedups and slowdowns, follow business activity.

Another group, the money stocks, are governed by money conditions. They include banks, insurance companies, and savings and loans. Their raw material is money, and here again a positive or negative yield spread is the governing factor, their dividends rising and falling with money rates. Public utilities have become money stocks—although they began in the pre-1949 era as the hottest growth stocks then in reach—because they rely on massive and repeated borrowings to finance continuous expansion.

The natural resource stocks represent wealth in the ground. The two important factors in their attractiveness are their particular raw material, plus low labor costs. Investors who regard labor inflation as the enemy do *not* want to own the stocks of construction companies—their search wants to be for stocks in industries where labor is a marginal cost of production. Natural resources meet this need.

There is a by-play to be looked at in buying natural resource stocks, however, and that is the political risk involved when the raw material is obtained abroad. Nickel in Nigeria, for example, was not a safe bet before or during the Biafran upheaval. Copper companies whose production is based on mines in Africa or South America are not the investment they would be if they were mining in North America.

Every sector of the stock market has its blue chip. But every blue chip has "blue chippies" in its shadow; on the fringe of every I.B.M. there is a Leasco. The emergence of a blue chippie is a second- or third-grade reaction to the success of the chips qualifying for investor confidence.

And behind the blue chippies are the "Cats and Dogs," the junk. When the ferryboat comes into the dock, it brings garbage in its wake. There are stock peddlers who, seeing U.S. Steel go up 20 percent, look around for a peripheral steel mill that can be sent shooting up even further. There have been little nickel stocks that have shot up by 300 to 400 percent—the "penny" stock markets in Canada and Australia are full of them. Stocks of under-financed and over-publicized franchise operations, together with garage laboratories whose names ended in "-onics," were the highest-flying junk in the American markets before the whistle blew for the great reckoning.

The movement of particular stocks, of particular groups of stocks, and of particular stock averages, is often misleading as to the general trend of the market as a whole. The professionals prefer to eye the so-called breadth index—the ratio of daily advances to declines—to provide a representative count of improvement or deterioration in the overall structure of the stock market. I think they are right.

The highest risk action in the stock market does not take place on the "big board," the New York Stock Exchange. The American Stock Exchange, too, has its quota of "chippie" entries. The Over-the-Counter market, where trading takes place in unlisted stocks, is where some of the biggest money was made and lost during the market swings of the 1960s.

One rule to remember comes into play when the rumor mills buzz with the word that an over-the-counter stock is about to be listed. This invariably spells bad news for the unwary, not good news. The reason is that so long as stocks are sequestered in the relative obscurity of the over-the-counter market, the insiders are content to hold their positions. Their motive in seeking listing on one of the exchanges is to attract buyers to cover their intention of cashing in their chips.

High risk has often given way to questionable practice when it comes to the next sector of the equity market— the underwriting of new issues. The placement of stock issues for privately owned companies ready for the big time as public corporations has long been one of the stock market's basic and economically most useful functions. But the abuse of the new-issue market invited outright market rigging, which consisted, to begin with, of marketing a small issue at a low price and rationing big fund buyers down to ridiculously small quotas of as little as a few hundred shares per buyer at the low issue price. The operation then assumed that each big buyer allowed to take, say, 500 of the new issue at $11, would follow the new offering onto the market with a buy order for five or ten thousand shares—a market, which, little wonder, invariably responded by building up into a quick hot boil.

The most extreme form this abuse took was the "letter" stock scandal. Mutual funds subject to redemptions by their own shareholders picked up disturbingly large amounts of unregistered and therefore legally unmarketable stock. This "letter" stock was invariably bought at bargain discounts and immediately marked up to its purely nominal face value. The gunslingers took their management fees for performance as if the paper mark-up measured a real price in market value. This is how the gunslingers looked like geniuses as they competed for places in Wall Street's Hall of Fame and "citations" in Adam Smith's *Money Game.*

Stocks traded over-the-counter, let alone new issues, are for professionals who know the risks, not for amateurs. Small investors will do well to remember the story that first convulsed the Wall Street pros with laughter and then left them weeping when the bell tolled for them:

After months of bidding for a hot number that seemed to set a new high every day, a do-it-yourself gunslinger finally suggested to the broker who had tipped him to buy the stock, "Why don't we sell a little and take some profit? I don't want to be greedy." "Sell it?" the broker asked. "To whom?"

Q. How do you rate the old-line blue chips versus the glamour stocks?

Mr. C. C. B. (*Oakland, California*)

A. The demoralization that has hit the stock market is separating the men from the boys. The boys are turning their backs on the stock fashions of their own creation. The men are starting to take a hard look at the bargains beginning to turn up in the securities of companies which have not only a past but a future and which, more than incidentally, have enough money in the bank to tide them over in the present.

As recently as spring, 1969, while the market swingers were still exploiting the fashion show, they were sneering at how square it was to be interested in old-line blue chips like General Motors. A remark by one of the most flamboyant characters satirized in Adam Smith's *Money Game* caught the spirit of that era: "General Motors is a stock to have inherited, not to buy." But suddenly the old rules have replaced the new. Yesterday's stock spectaculars, which were held together by twigs, have fallen apart for lack of the glue that only liquidity can provide when money is tight; and stocks that the young fund managers had priced up out of sight are going bidless.

By the same token, the stocks of the big companies, which were "out" while money seemed unimportant, are becoming "in" again now that stocks with money behind them are again commanding a bigger premium than stocks with stories presumed to be in front of them.

Q. What has happened to I.B.M.?

> *Mr. J. A. W. (Indianapolis, Indiana)*

A. "Mystique" is defined by Webster's new international dictionary as "the special esoteric skill or mysterious faculty essential in a calling or activity."

This is the word that describes the aura I.B.M. has projected across the stock market during the entire era of confidence upon which Wall Street is now looking back. So commanding, indeed, has been I.B.M.'s grip on the imagination of the financial world that its magic initials have long been accepted as symbolizing a new leadership role in the stock market.

Another word, simpler in everyday usage but also involving magic in money-making, has told a more specific story about I.B.M.'s stock market leadership. The word is *growth*. Once I.B.M. came to typify the idea of growth, the idea began to sprout an altogether new family of junior I.B.M.s—Xerox, Polaroid, Litton, Control Data, and Syntex. Membership in this exclusive "growth stock" club has remained open to new entries. American Research and Development is one that took advantage of the standing invitation to crash the gates. But membership is also subject to high risks corresponding to the high stakes for which members in the growth club play. Control Data became a conspicuous casualty before trouble caught up with the group as a whole.

The traumatic drop in the growth group took over downside market leadership from the more stolid, workhorse stocks rating inclusion in the Dow-Jones Industrial Average. What is surprising about the stir caused by the trouble which has overcome the growth group is that it came as a surprise.

Leverage, after all, is well known to be a two-way street. The human race had the benefit of common sense for centuries on end before there was a stock market or stock market experts; and common sense teaches us to expect anything that goes up faster while it's still going up to come down faster after it has started coming down.

The market trouble in I.B.M. started with a humdrum interim earnings report. The numbers do not matter. What does matter is that the report made it official that no company in America—not even I.B.M.—is exempt from the deflation which today's inflation has been visiting upon earnings.

Q. *I fail to see the logic of selling proven growth stocks like I.B.M., Xerox, and N.C.R. just because the stock market is being hurt by the distress of companies which are not outrunning the pack as these are. Inasmuch as you seem to agree, despite your stock market pessimism, that these growth companies will continue to grow faster than everything else, how do you explain your recommendation that the growth leaders be sold, too?*

Mr. K. B. R. (New York City, New York)

A. The new rule of the road in the disaster area spanned by Wall Street now grades stocks by the ability of sellers to find buyers and it is only top-grade stocks that are being bid for as freely as they are being offered. The money squeeze has put stockholders under the gun to turn their paper into cash—if they can. And those that are owners of the best-grade stocks sell them because they can find buyers to bid for them.

This of course has created the paradox whereby the stocks of higher investment quality are going down faster than stocks of lower investment quality. No stocks have suffered more abrupt and breathtaking collapses in recent months than the very best-grade growth stocks, like I.B.M. They can be freely sold and buyers are willing to bid for them at prices calculated to deflate values and reflect the toll the inflationary erosion has taken of their earning power. The weaker sisters are the ones enjoying a misleading stability on the surface of the market, and they are not going down for the simple reason that their sellers cannot find buyers.

Q. Why should an investor buy utility stocks?

Mr. A. A. H. (*Kalamazoo, Michigan*)

A. As I have stressed many times in the past, utility stocks are wonderful vehicles for long-term investment—especially for beneficial accounts for children and grandchildren—because their dividends are stable and can be counted on to rise regularly, so that over a span of years, regardless of fluctuations from easy money to tight money and from good business to poor business, the values underlying utility stocks are bound to register steady, if gradual, gain.

But if safety of dividend and assurance of long-term growth are the reasons for sitting it out with utility stocks during the inflationary squeeze, the reason not to buy utility stocks until the squeeze is broken is that they are money stocks. Consequently, they are sensitive to the negative yield spread. This means that when the yield offered by their bonds is nearly twice that of their dividends, investors understandably switch from their stocks to their bonds.

In the summer of 1970 the Illinois Public Service Commission provided yet another reason for downgrading the pluses in favor of utility stocks against the minuses. It awarded the top-rated Commonwealth Edison a rate increase but put it on notice that half the increase would be forfeited unless the company put up hard cash at a rate stipulated to engineer pollution out of its plant. Related regulatory hazards in other states are dramatizing the difficulty which utilities are having in fighting the two-front war against blackouts and pollution.

It is axiomatic that the utilities are on the losing side of the time lag in any period of inflation. This time around, regulatory hazards are lengthening the time lag. Again and again, utilities are hit with new costs before they can get their own back.

Q. A few weeks ago you wrote an article about utility stocks being tax-deductible. I would like to know exactly what type of stock you mean, and how much is deductible.

Mr. J. G. (Elmwood Park, Illinois)

A. Utility stocks are not "tax-deductible," but a portion of the dividends they pay may be non-taxable. Many utility stocks with excellent growth records pay relatively low returns that are entirely taxable. The tax-free feature of the dividend from any particular stock varies from year to year with the amount of depreciation a utility company is allowed to take on its rate base. Depreciation creates a book loss and, depending on the amount taken, all or part of the dividend is treated as if it is not a payment of earnings. All brokers have lists of tax-sheltered utility dividends.

Q. I am 67, single, no dependents. Over the last 40 years I have accumulated blue-chip oil and utility stocks, and the value of these has more than doubled. During the past two years, I have bought short-term A-rated bonds yielding 7.6 percent. Now I would like to switch my stocks

*into more bonds, but the tax bite on the profits would
probably be greater than any fall in stock prices. What do
you suggest I do?*

Mr. J. A. B. (*Elmhurst, Illinois*)

A. The run-up in interest rates is a major reason for
stock market jeopardy, and because the utility stocks are
primarily money stocks, they are top candidates for sale
in any period of money trouble. This is so even though
the young investor today who buys blue-chip utilities to
hold for 40 years will probably do as well with them as
you have over the past 40 years. Your high-yielding bonds
probably show some losses; you could use them to offset
stock profits taken. Thus you could switch from stocks
to bonds and also improve your bond yields.

The oils divide into two main groups: those primarily
international, and those which are North American based.
Those vulnerable to a Middle Eastern crisis are in the
most jeopardy. The kind of market break that we have
experienced—a break precipitated by inflationary war
spending and inflationary interest rates—is likely to favor
the asset stocks over the glamour stocks. You'll do well to
hold your big North American oil stocks.

As to the tax consequences of profit-taking, the first rule
of the road to bear in mind is that anyone with profits in
a falling market is ahead of the game taking them. The
second rule, which your record qualifies you to master, is
that the "spill-over" tax shelter afforded by direct investment in property (and described in Chapter IV) can be
used to offset capital gains taken on stocks no longer having anywhere to go but down.

Q. Do you think that a complete or partial cutoff of Middle Eastern oil is possible? If so, how seriously would this affect international oil stocks? Also, are foreign economic and political difficulties amply discounted in the current prices of oil shares? I own an international oil and, although I am just about even, I am worried.

Mr. F. J. S. (Northbrook, Illinois)

A. My best judgment is that no market adjustment could amply discount the political dangers overhanging traditional oil values in the Middle East.

Even if shooting does not flare up again, the Russians appear to have established their political primacy throughout the Middle Eastern oil country. Between Arab nationalism and Soviet imperialism the international oil companies are going to be under endless pressure to raise immeasurable sums of new high cost capital to replace their low cost Middle Eastern reserves. The stocks of companies in need of new money invariably come under selling pressure.

While there have been recurrent short-term plays in the international oils, I think that the longer-term risks outweigh the incentives to take this chance.

Why not take advantage of any speculative run-up to get out of your international oil into a quality domestic oil? The market in American oil shares is benefiting from the troubles plaguing the international oils; and it will continue to do so.

Q. I am a 32-year-old father of two sons aged six and four. My wife and I are trying to accumulate education funds for them.

During the last 18 months we have purchased a few hundred shares of oil shale stock which I feel will be of value in 10 to 12 years.

Mr. I. D. (Portland, Oregon)

A. There is no doubt whatever that America's rich shale-oil reserves represent a major source of growth earning power for the future; and it is my judgment that we are rapidly approaching the point at which it will become necessary for the Interior Department to open the Government's oil-bearing shale lands to oil company use. But the economic way to invest in this growth potential is through the securities of major oil companies with a head start on this phase of the art, not by taking fliers on the speculative stocks of smaller companies lacking the needed capital. The shale-minded investor who makes his play on the future in major oil company securities will be well paid for waiting, but shale will be a very expensive game to get into. It's not for small players or for quick fliers.

Q. You have said that life insurance stocks won't regain their highs of a few years ago until there is a return to lower interest rates. But life insurance companies are lenders of money and not borrowers, and it seems to me that they should benefit from the higher interest rates. Where is my reasoning wrong?

Mr. C. F. (East Aurora, New York)

A. It's too simplistic. "Money stocks"—banks, savings and loans, insurance companies, finance companies—rise when the price of the commodity they have to sell falls. Why should this be any more confusing than that Henry Ford bought profitable volume when he cut his prices? Insurance companies lend money, but the money they lend they have to borrow. They are paying high prices for money when policyholders are exercising their right to get cheap money loans from them.

Also they are long-term lenders. Massive portions of their portfolios are committed at long-term, and when investment availability gets tight, they find themselves unable to take advantage of the chance to lend money out at high rates because so much of their assets were committed when rates were low. They find themselves getting 6 percent for money in a 12 percent market. The squeeze works against them in another way, too, by producing bankruptcies in which they get caught.

Q. Would you please comment on bank stocks and what causes their gyrations.

Mr. G. M. (Chicago, Illinois)

A. Bank stocks can fool you. They tend to fall during periods of high interest rates when their earnings rise and to rise when rates fall. Substantial local investors tend to accumulate bank stocks when they get worried about general conditions and when bank stocks sell at low price-earnings ratios. Bank stocks are good buys toward the end of a tight money cycle. The bank stocks are the one major group that rises in price when the commodity they have to sell falls in price.

Q. On a number of occasions you have suggested buying stock in suburban banks. What is your reason for this recommendation?

> *Miss E. K. B. (Morton Grove, Illinois)*

A. The big city banks suffer from chronic shortages of liquidity—both because their big business customers need so much money and because the Federal Reserve Board is so erratic about drying up their lending power whenever the heat is on to "fight inflation." But the inflation is manufacturing liquidity as fast as it is creating liquidity shortages and dislocations. And the liquidity in the money system is gravitating toward the country banks.

Moreover, the country banks rate as one of the most steadily—and safely—growing businesses in the country. There are many businesses with high liquidity and no growth, and there are many with high growth and no liquidity. Put the two together, and you have something to prize.

A final reason for favoring country bank stocks is that they tend to attract loyal followings of local investors. After all, what makes stocks go up is more than just earnings. It takes more money from willing buyers.

Q. From my 15-year experience in the market, I have learned that patience and not trying to buy at rock-bottom prices are vital to investment success.

But, looking ahead to the early '70s, I have concluded that buying insurance stocks during the next year could prove rewarding, because insurance companies will benefit from their investments in high interest bonds, many of which are noncallable for several years. Have I reached the right conclusion?

Mr. H. R. H. (Arlington Heights, Illinois)

A. Three breeds of animal roam the Wall Street jungle —the bulls, the bears, and the pigs. Congratulations on not running with the third pack. The vultures always get them.

Looking forward to the early 1970s, I agree with your judgment about insurance stocks. Because time is money, however, timing is all-important in investment; and, as the continuing rise in interest rates reminds us, money and the time spent waiting for it are worth a premium. Insurance stocks are not likely to come back into their own until the cost of their raw material—money—comes back down to supportable levels.

Q. My portfolio consists of the natural resource stocks on the enclosed list. I am not just waiting on them for safety until the market makes bottom. I believe there will be a flow of money into these types of issues. I am 26 and do not have the patience to put my money in real estate or the nerve to buy silver futures. Are my positions facing too many risks to hold?

Mr. D. A. M. (Chicago, Illinois)

A. I like your sense of direction, although I am worried about your selectivity—and certainly not because I worry about young fellows of 26 who have earnings and who are willing to speculate. In fact, you are insuring your speculations by being frank to admit that that is exactly what you are doing.

The only quality security you have is a metals processor, which—while it happens to be an extremely well-managed company—does not qualify as an owner of natural resources in a politically safe area.

I agree with you that there will be a flow of money into natural resource stocks and into stocks close to natural resources. But I don't think you have found them. I also think that your timing is reckoning without the length of time I feel it will take for the bear market money squeeze to unwind.

Q. You have been distinguishing between the performance of speculatively managed mutual funds and conservatively managed ones. Presumably the conservative funds have been assiduously accumulating cash and cash equivalents during the months of distress, and holding on to their prime-grade equities. But do you know of any groups of stocks to which they have felt free to commit money since the onset of the bear market?

Mrs. A. H. B. (Bethel, Connecticut)

A. Your question is well formulated and your presumptions realistic. On the positive side, the leading conservative funds have been aggressive buyers of the natural gas stocks. These are natural resource stocks par excellence and, moreover, represent a natural resource in acute short supply—so much so that the regulatory authorities have no alternative but to sanction sharp increases in rates.

The industry is capital intensive and, therefore, enjoys the benefit of large, long-term bonded indebtedness. An incidental plus is that the natural gas producers have traditionally shown themselves more sophisticated in dealing with the Washington "alphabet" agencies than other industries subject to regulatory supervision.

Q. From your writings, I gather you are opposed to conglomerates. Will you explain why?

Mrs. J. E. C. (*Dallas, Texas*)

A. Conglomerates were market leaders, less because of the businesses they took over than because they were in the take-over business when the market was a market in take-over stocks. But as fast as confidence was encouraged in the stock market performance of the conglomerates, doubts arose lest they might prove more professional in moving stocks upward than in engineering sound corporate vehicles and in fielding strong management teams able to move themselves forward. Also, increasingly, the process of conglomeration gave birth to operational misfits with managements rushing into fields they knew nothing about. The simplest explanation of their collapse was that they resorted to unsound practices in their headlong rush to grow by acquisition, without regard to how much they paid to buy how much genuine earning power.

But the main reason the conglomerates forfeited the market's confidence can be summed up in one word, "excessivism." While conglomeration was in vogue, it went too far, too fast, too recklessly and, in the end, too provocatively. The market, already worried about overspeculation in general, took fright over conglomerate speculation in particular and put the conglomerates down long before Washington counted them out.

Q. Aerospace stocks have been falling steadily. All of these companies have introduced new products that should increase their sales volume and should indicate strength instead of weakness, even in a bear market. How come they're going down?

Mr. R. P. C. (Seattle, Washington)

A. The inflationary cost squeeze has raised risks and costs for establishing new products; it has lengthened the time needed to get a payback on them; and it has lowered the rate of return. This goes double for the advanced technology field, for two reasons: it is capital-intensive, which makes financing unprofitable; and Government is the major customer, which makes profit unlikely. The airlines are the other customer; and, in their strained condition, this makes for slim sales pickings.

Q. Would the major commercial airline stocks be a good buy for capital appreciation over the next five years or so?

Mr. E. B. E. (Cleveland, Ohio)

A. I doubt it. The money crisis reversed the rules that put a premium on growth while the bull market was still on. Now, instead, the greater the growth an industry is involved in financing, the greater the disadvantage the big companies in it are obliged to operate under. I am inclined to think the airline stocks are so bound up with the main trend of the economy that they will not make their lows until the market does—after the money squeeze is ended. The backlash from Penn Central cast a pall over the whole transportation sector of the market, subject as it is to the cost-squeeze in general, to capital-raising in particular—and to the blight of over-regulation.

The squeeze on the airline stocks dramatizes the switch from an investment plus into an investment minus in the growth sector. The increased chanciness of the carriers' expectations of cost-plussing their price structure is becoming a more and more erratic consideration. Airlines are now subject to the rate-raising difficulties of utilities. The political resistance to inflation spells bad news for the stocks of all companies subject to regulation over their price levels.

Q. We are in our early forties and have three young children. We became interested in atomic power 9 years ago and bought some uranium stock. Watching the continued growth of atomic power has been a hobby with us—one that we hesitate to give up. But we would do so if it seemed advisable to pay off our mortgage. What would you do?

Mr. R. W. M. (Nappanee, Indiana)

A. Quality investment in the long-term growth of uranium and nuclear power values represents a more economic use of funds than freezing cash in mortgage repayment.

Q. In view of the breathtaking increases in health costs, and the fact that both the Government and corporate pension funds are putting up so much money to foot the bills, why aren't nursing home stocks good "buy" bets in spite of all the trouble the big stocks are in?

Mr. A. M. (New York City, New York)

A. Your observation is realistic, but your reasoning is not. It runs smack into the rule that companies whose business is great need even more cash than companies whose business is punk. All the nursing home stocks have speculative allure because the demand for commercial health services is rising faster than anyone can count. Don't expect the stock of any company needing to raise new money in a sick capital market to act healthy. Let the bankruptcy of IOS-backed Four Seasons—until yesterday a "hot" nursing home stock—point the moral: growth and demand do not guarantee investment appreciation.

Q. I am thinking of buying some medical electronic stocks, as their future prospects seem bright. What do you think of that field?

Mr. J. B. (Skokie, Illinois)

A. The field is tremendous. Good demand is way ahead of capacities, so that the high cost of technological research and development is easier to finance in this field than in others. Just be sure that you don't gamble on companies not likely to make it. With prospects so favorable for the companies that are, there's no need to speculate. The market leaders in the health-products field are well financed, and are likelier bets to do well than new starters.

Q. Do you think that pharmaceutical stock is a good investment now?

Mrs. D. B. (Omaha, Nebraska)

A. The more profitable a pharmaceutical company is today, the more vulnerable its price structure and public relations are to regulatory sandbagging. Also, the most dynamic American pharmaceutical companies are most dependent on foreign investment and foreign borrowing, and this is in a money bind. I'd hold off.

Q. *I am a young physician and although I have managed to learn a little medicine, I must confess to a large dose of ignorance concerning matters of economics. In view of present international monetary reform problems, I wonder whether you feel it advisable to maintain a percentage of one's investable funds in gold shares, as a hedge against the future instability and possible devaluation of the dollar.*

G. M. G., M.D. (Chicago, Illinois)

A. Golds are the most speculative of stocks because they are more dependent than any other on the whim of government. The American Government could break the price of gold or, at least, end the speculation on a higher price which gold stock players are betting on. Incidentally, doctors rank with clergymen, soldiers, and teachers as notorious market losers.

Americans cannot buy gold legally. Those who can in Europe incur onerous interest costs with no return except the emotional satisfaction they get from the aura of owning gold. There are only two reasons for Americans to buy gold stocks. The first is a speculation on a higher official price for gold. This is a mug's game. The second is mass pessimism on the market. Gold stocks move against such massive swings of emotion. This is a pro's game.

Q. Ordinarily, I quite agree with your opinions. However, I find that I must take issue with your recent column in which you group all Canadian stocks categorically as "not worth buying." Seven years ago I invested in one of the baby blue chips among the Canadian industrials. Since then, this stock has not only doubled in value and paid good dividends, but it also held its own in the recent bear market. I am sure that there are other good Canadian stocks, too.

Mr. C. F. M. (Grand Island, New York)

A. Glad to know that you agree with my judgments in general. Perhaps you would agree with my judgment on Canadian market performance, too, if only you would reread what I said in full: "When Americans don't buy Canadian stocks (and they aren't now), Canadian stocks aren't worth buying."

Not only do I agree that there are good Canadian stocks; I believe that the best Canadian values are second to none anywhere. But without buyers and hard cash buying, even the best stocks sell at deep discounts under their underlying values. It is one of the facts of market life that it takes American buying to move Canadian stock prices.

Q. I often see you recommending property as an investment. Do you think property stocks are a good buy as well?

Mr. A. B. L. (Hartford, Connecticut)

A. Theoretically they would be the very best. The practical pitfalls, however, are just as obvious as the theoretical attractions.

Securities buyable as property stocks fall into two groups. The first comprises well-established companies in other lines of work which happen to have rich property holdings accumulated years ago at no cost and therefore presumably resalable at rich discounts from present market values.

The most obvious example of property-rich asset values deemed to be going at deep discounts is offered by the railroads; and indeed the knee-jerk reaction of money analysts to the prognosis of higher land values and advantages offered by property accumulation is to buy rail stocks. But while Western railroads in particular have an empire of undeveloped acreage reflected in their balance sheets, which offers enormous potential for future development, unfortunately, none of them have the managerial "oomph" to maximize this second string to their bow.

The other main group is the aggressive land development companies. Just as the property-rich rails are handicapped by their unimaginative and unaggressive managements, so the aggressive promotion-minded managements of land companies are offset by the vulnerability of land development to inflationary squeezes on the credit and labor markets.

The high cost of construction puts obvious hurdles in the way of converting land from its raw state into housing. The intermediate cost of developing and preparing land for construction—providing sewage, roads, and utilities—is particularly high. It involves long-lead times between investment and payback. Moreover, once income-producing construction is put in place, it generally has to be sold on the installment plan, subject to small down-payments—large accumulations of receivables of dubious quality and virtually no bankability. This means that land development companies, while rich in paper earnings, are short of cash. The richer they are in paper, the shorter they are of cash.

By investing in property stocks you run up against the kind of risks I recommend avoiding by buying property itself. But one of these days a management in the property business will develop the investment answer to avoid these risks. On the day the market sees it, and finds it durable, that precious rarity, a bear market growth stock, will be launched. Meanwhile, anticipating such a launching, the big new development in the mutual fund field centers on the setting up of funds that enable the small investor to buy direct participation in property assets in the form of fund shares. This investment idea, like so many others copied in America, is already well along in Britain.

Q. Investment commentators always talk about which stock groups to buy. How can I tell which particular stock to buy?

Mr. D. V. A. (New York City, New York)

A. Look at the balance sheet. We are in a balance sheet market, and no matter which sector of the market looks good for the short term, when it comes to the stocks of individual companies, the name of the game is look at the balance sheet.

CHAPTER VIII

Bonds

THE stock market has been in an admitted bear market of major proportions since 1968, but the bond market has been getting its lumps since 1948. In the last few years it has been suffering a private 1929 of its own. As it has fallen, it has attracted a new consensus among the silent majority whose members are steadily casting their pocketbook votes on the side of bonds. Inveterate savers and former stock-chasers alike are putting their four- and five-figure accumulations into this income-getting paper.

Whether or not they are premature or realistic in their timing or how close the battered bond market may be to bottom and, therefore, how close today's inflated rates of return may be to topping out, they think they are getting fair value for their money. They may very well be making more sense with their dollars than those who have remained stuck in stocks.

At the same time, governments and businesses all over the country—from Main Street to Wall Street—are competing to raise badly needed cash by selling bonds on an increasingly large scale, providing rich opportunities for the saver and investor.

Bonds are long-term obligations to pay a fixed number of dollars in interest each year, and a fixed number of dollars—the principal—back at the end of a specified time. The interest rate is based on the face value of the bond, generally $1,000, so that the amount of dollars paid during its life is almost always fixed in advance.

A bond that guarantees the payment of $50 per year in interest until it matures, for example, has what is termed a nominal interest rate of 5 percent. If it matures in twenty years, the holders of the bond during its life will have received $1,000 in interest payments by the time it matures and will then receive the $1,000 of principal. If interest rates fall, bond issuers will want to redeem their outstanding bonds bearing high interest rates in order to borrow at lower cost. When interest rates are high, investors demand—and get—"call protection" against early redemption of new issues, often for 5 to 10 years on 20- to 30-year bonds.

Bonds come in a variety of shapes and from a variety of borrowers. Corporations—above all, public utilities— and state and local governments are the biggest issuers, because they make the biggest long-term capital investments.

The Federal Government also issues bonds—when it can. It hasn't been able to do so—on the table, at least— for some years because of a statutory ceiling on the interest rate the U.S. Treasury can pay on debt with a maturity of more than seven years. The only legal, simple way the Treasury can borrow at long term today is through the E-bond swindle, about which more below: more below, too, on the stratagem the Federal Government has devised to obtain "back door" long-term money through "debudgeted" agencies.

Many state and local governments also face interest ceilings, but their interest payments to investors are tax-free, unlike those of the Treasury and corporations. These ceilings have only restricted long-term municipal borrowings in the past two years.

Bonds are issued not only to finance long-term capital investment. They are also issued in order to "fund" accumulated short-term borrowings. The demand for long-term money in the first half of 1970—that is, the backlog of bond issues ready to come to market—was made up in large part from borrowers of all varieties who either could not legally borrow at recent market interest rates or who trusted their "expert" advice that interest rates would come down soon, and substantially. Despite a record volume of bond issues for the past year, short-term debts remained enormous and so did the need to issue bonds.

The market constantly adjusts the value of outstanding bonds to bring the nominal interest rate on outstanding bonds—the rate shown on the coupon—into line with the current rate on new issues. If interest rates go up, the prices of outstanding bonds will go down, and if interest rates go down, bond prices will go up. For example, if the interest rate on newly issued bonds is 10 percent, the market value of an old $1,000 bond paying 5 percent will adjust downwards toward $500. The result will be that an investor, after the price adjustment, will be able to get the same $100 yield on a $1,000 investment either by buying one new bond yielding 10 percent at its face value or two old bonds yielding 5 percent at half their face value.

No matter how far the price of a bond falls during the course of its life—how deep a "discount" the market puts on a bond—at maturity the holder of the bond is entitled to its full face value. This leads to two different ways of calculating the value of the income received by the purchaser of a bond. The "current yield" is simply derived by dividing the annual interest payment by the current market price of the bond. The "yield to maturity" takes into account the capital gain—the difference between current price and face value—that the purchaser will receive if he holds the bond until it matures, as well as the interest payment.

Because interest payments are generally taxed at full rates as ordinary income, while capital gains accrued over a period of more than six months are taxed at substantially lower rates, "deep-discount" bonds—most of whose yield to maturity is accounted for by capital gains—can be particularly attractive on an after-tax basis. If interest rates on new issues are likely to fall sharply, thus raising the market price on outstanding bonds and providing their holders with capital gains, deep-discount bonds can be attractive even if the purchaser does not intend to hold them to maturity.

Interest rates on new issues tend to rise for two fundamental reasons. The first is to discount present and future inflation; thus, today's 9 to 10 percent interest rates leave the interest recipient, after inflation, with about the same 3 to 4 percent return he received back in the old days when prices were almost constant. Inflation still hurts fixed-income recipients, but less so when they are receiving interest rates of 10 percent than of 5 percent.

The second reason interest rates rise is to reflect a

growth in the general demand for capital relative to its supply. This has clearly been a factor in the great drive upwards in interest rates during the 1960s, as bonds have been issued to finance massive programs of public and private investment.

Aside from "straight debt," described above, corporate borrowers can also issue "convertible debentures." "Convertibles" pay interest at a fixed rate on a fixed sum. But they also have an "equity kicker": at some specified future time they are convertible into the stock of the issuer. When the stock market is rising and, therefore, is expected to continue rising, corporations can borrow by issuing convertibles more cheaply—but at the cost of diluting their stockholders in the future—than they can by issuing bonds. When the stock market falls out of bed, convertibles hit the floor first.

A "little brother" to convertible debentures is preferred stock which, although it is called a stock, is really more like a bond. It confers voting rights on its owner plus a fixed dividend which is guaranteed payment before that on common stock. Preferred stocks are less attractive than convertible debentures when convertibles are attractive, but they are also less vulnerable when convertibles are vulnerable.

Bonds can be purchased when issued and held to maturity, at which time they will be redeemed at face value, or they can be bought and sold at any time, very much as stocks are, through brokers. But the broker's commission on bonds is less than that on stocks, which is why few brokers are willing to trade them for small customers.

Traditionally, the bond investor is the investor for income, but the bond market also serves as the speculator's market par excellence. Unlike the stock market, it is a happy hunting ground for the professional speculator who operates on a big scale and on a small margin of his own money.

Timing is the key to successful bond market speculation—timing of drops in interest rates. Bond prices jump when interest rates drop. When big-time speculators make money in changes in bond market direction, they make more money than anyone else ever makes in stocks. Reason: when banks are looking for loans, bonds are easier to borrow against than stocks. With a 5 percent margin, only $50,000 of cash will buy a speculator (who is big enough to have bank credit) $1 million in Government bonds; the other $950,000 is put up by the bank as a loan. The professional speculator can double his money with only a 5-point rise in market price.

Both the amateur and the professional are earning record returns in the bond market, while providing a seemingly endless source of funds for governments and businesses. By buying bonds *after* it has sold stocks, the public is putting its past record for making sense about money behind the future of the dollar. It is betting that the fixed annual income to be earned on bonds, which has reached unprecedentedly high levels, will not all be eaten up by the continued acceleration of inflation. The rate of return on a bond is fixed and, therefore, the bet on a high yield to insure against continuing inflation remains a bet that inflation will be checked within a reasonable amount of time. Meanwhile, as a practical matter, the 1969-1970 switch into bonds from stocks—the traditional but now discredited inflation hedge—has already spelled more bad news for the stock market, but good news for Main Street and for the country and its economy.

Q. How are bond prices quoted? What are "premiums" and "discounts" on bonds?

Mrs. V. N. R. (Denver, Colorado)

A. Bond quotations are based on 100 as equal to par, the face value of the bond. The prices quoted on outstanding bonds are adjusted upwards or downwards in the bond market as interest rates on new issues fall or rise. The premium in the quoted price of a bond is the percentage amount above par that a purchaser will have to pay for it; conversely, the discount on a bond is the percentage amount below the face value that a purchaser will pay. A bond with a face value of $1,000 quoted at 90 will cost a purchaser $900.

The great majority of bonds outstanding in 1970 have been quoted at discounts, because of the sustained rise in interest rates over the whole postwar period, a rise that accelerated in the second half of the 1960s. In looking for the yield on discount bonds, remember that the "yield to maturity" takes into account the fact that, whatever the price paid for a bond, the full face value—the par value— is due at maturity. This is why the price rises (and the discount falls) as the date of maturity nears. This appreciation in price, which reaches 100 at maturity no matter how far below current interest rates the nominal rate on the bond is, is taxed as capital gains. Given the low tax rate on capital gains, deep-discount bonds with good ratings have become attractive investments to hold as their date of maturity approaches. Deep-discount bonds can also be expected to rise in price sharply as and when interest rates head back down to tolerable levels. They and their owners will be the first beneficiaries of a re-assertion of control over America's runaway crisis of inflation and illiquidity.

One caveat. Extraordinarily deep discounts on bonds reflect the market's professional judgment that there is a more or less serious risk that the issuer will be unable to meet interest payments or to redeem the bonds at maturity. The prices quoted on Penn Central bonds are a case in point. For a really extreme example, there is even a market in Tsarist bonds—which trade for pennies per thousand dollars—on the far-out chance that they may someday be redeemed by the Kremlin! "Super deep"-discount bonds are outright speculations, not investments. The financial pressures that drove the Penn Central to seek "the protection of the courts" have placed a discount on the bonds of any issuer whose financial position is suspect. That is why a wide gap has opened up, for the first time since the 1930s, between the yields on top-rated issues (A and upward) and lower-rated issues. The gap exists both for new issues and for outstanding bonds.

When a bankruptcy actually does happen and the bonds of the bankrupt corporation become totally speculative, until the court works out which of the creditors get what, the trustees issue trustee certificates. These are a sound investment, so sound that they are limited to bank use. Not until after the financial landscape has been strewn with bankruptcies do major capital gains opportunities reappear in "reorganization" rail bonds. This was a big opportunity during the first stages of the late bull market.

Old-timers who did well out of the last bust are hoping that the rule-rutted Interstate Commerce Commission will give them another chance to clean up on another crop of busted railroads. Their intellectual heirs are hoping that the Civil Aeronautics Board will give them an even juicier whack at a line-up of busted airlines.

Q. Which do you recommend, short- or long-term bonds? Would you explain why one is better than the other?

Mrs. J. D. (Tucson, Arizona)

A. Any use of bonds involves a speculation on interest rates and on inflation. Short-term bonds won't yield quite as high a rate of return as long-term bonds, but they will minimize the exposure to still further increases in interest rates, as well as to further inflation. The investor in short-term bonds need not worry about depreciation in market value because of the assurance that repayment will be made in full in a relatively short time.

But investment in long-term bonds that are protected against call for a substantial number of years is particularly rewarding after a protracted period of rising interest rates because it assures the investor a peak rate of return after yields have begun to fall. The time to go whole-hog in long-term bonds is when interest rates are peaking.

Q. I know the Federal Government is always borrowing money. The financial pages report on the sale of Treasury bills, and I understand that these are short-term, up to one year. How does the Treasury borrow for longer periods?

Mr. R. E. T. (Detroit, Michigan)

A. The Treasury also issues notes and bonds. Their notes are medium-term debt instruments with an average maturity of five years, and bonds are long-term carrying a maturity of up to 30 years. It sells both notes and bonds whenever it can find buyers willing to hold its paper as investments in income or as a speculation on lower interest rates, rather than as interest-bearing cash equivalents, which is what Treasury bills are.

And whereas Treasury bills are virtually riskless, the longer-term notes and bonds are not. For the investor, risks lie in the rate of inflation; for the speculator, in changes in interest rates.

I would not recommend Government bonds as investments. Professional speculators play with them on thin margins when they expect interest rates to drop. This is not investment.

Q. I have between $3,000 and $5,000 that I want to invest for income. I was thinking of buying U.S. Treasury notes due in 1977, paying around 8 percent. What is the difference between U.S. Treasury bonds, bills, and notes? And what is the advantage of buying notes?

Mr. C. W. (St. Petersburg, Fla.)

A. U.S. Treasury notes bear much shorter maturities than bonds. They fill the gap between Treasury bills and bonds.

The advantage today's Treasury note holders have over

Treasury bond holders is due to present inflationary market conditions. Treasury note holders can earn the high going rate without being subject to paper losses because of further increases in long-term interest rates, while being assured of getting their money back in the next few years.

Treasury note holders have another advantage over Treasury bill holders due to the recent regulatory change which raised the minimum limit on Treasury bills to $10,000, but let the old $1,000 minimum remain in force on Treasury notes. The Government's purpose in raising the minimum limit on bill-buying was to stop the stampede of small savers from lower-yielding passbooks into Treasury bills. Now a new stampede seems to be starting in notes.

So long as Treasury notes remain buyable in $1,000 denominations, they seem on the way to becoming as popular with small savers as Treasury bills were before the limit was raised.

Q. You often advise people to buy Government agency bonds. Are they listed in the paper? What are some names? Do you buy them at a bank or from a broker?

Mr. D. L. P. (San Francisco, California)

A. These bonds are obligations of United States Government-controlled corporations and represent a device by the Treasury to peddle paper around through its "back door" which Congress prohibits it from offering through its front door.

Congress has imposed a 4¼ percent ceiling on direct obligations of the U.S. Treasury carrying maturities of over seven years. This is Congress's way of expressing its disapproval of high interest rates. The ceiling officially prevents the Treasury from lengthening its debt at the very time when it is putting maximum pressure on the short-term credit market, and, therefore, when it most needs to build long-term debt. But Government agencies and corporations like the TVA, FHA, Federal Land bank and Federal Home Loan bank are able to issue bonds.

Some of these bonds are guaranteed by the Government and some are not. All brokers' bond sheets list them and banks deal in them for their own account and for their investment advisory customers. But the way to buy them is through a securities dealer or broker. Before you give a broker the go-ahead, however, make sure he consults a lawyer about whether or not a particular bond is guaranteed, so that you know where you are.

Q. How and by whom are bonds rated?

Mrs. N. B. (Baton Rouge, Louisiana)

A. By objective and independent rating services, which go by set standards. The ultimate criterion of these standards measures the margin by which bond borrowers can be expected to cover their interest charges and their sinking-fund requirements.

Coverage of fixed charges is taken as a measure of likely ability not to default on interest payments or principal.

Ratings set the rule of the road in credit markets: corporations are sensitive and vigilant in avoiding downgrading in their ratings.

The interest rates bonds bear at issue vary with their ratings. The ratings, starting with the best and going down, are as follows:

Moody's—   Aaa, Aa, A, Baa, Ba, B, Caa, Ca, C.
Standard & Poor's   AAA, AA, A, DDD, DD, B, CCC-CC, C, DDD-D.

State and local governments, as well as corporations, are subject to this scrutiny and may be down-rated while they are outstanding—if the rating services decide that the coverage of interest is more rather than less risky. But the rating services are conservative, and any well-rated Government or corporate bond is safe as to interest and principal.

Q. What are AAA bonds, how much do they cost, and where may they be purchased? Plus anything that you think I might need to know about such a bond.

Miss F. M. (Chicago, Illinois)

A. AAA bonds are those enjoying top-quality ratings from the rating services. Bonds issued by the Telephone Company, its regional subsidiaries, and the top blue-chip utilities and industrials qualify. As a practical matter, buyers of AAA bonds over-pay for credit insurance: AA-rated bonds and even bonds with lower ratings are just as sure to pay their interest and meet their repayment schedules.

Traditionally the watershed has separated As from BBBs, the reason being that fiduciaries are barred from buying BBBs. But the credit squeeze has raised the level of the watershed, so that, increasingly, the cutoff point between bonds deemed to enjoy investment quality is between the AAs and the As. The transition is important because if a bond once suffers downgrading from A to BBB, its price is sure to tumble even faster than rising interest rates are forcing bond prices down anyway, and the terms subject to which it can be sold will become more unfavorable.

The way to figure what it costs to buy quality "money-good" bonds is purely and simply in terms of the yield their interest payments represent. When, for example, the going rate on new AAA issues is set by a 9½ percent coupon, a $1,000 investment will buy $95 of taxable income per annum. If the going rate on new issues rises to 10 percent, $1,000 will buy $100 of annual taxable income, and therefore a bond with a coupon rate of 9½ percent will be worth no more than $950 in the market.

Any bank or broker will buy bonds for you for a small fee.

Q. I am a doctor, and frequently I get information on the buying of hospital bonds. The yield is usually around 7 percent. Do you think it wise to invest in this type of bond, or should I stay strictly with Government-guaranteed bonds?

Dr. E. R. (Houston, Texas)

A. Investigate your hospital management before investing. Even the best-managed hospitals are being caught in the inflationary squeeze—although the selling of health services is probably America's number-one growth business. Bonds of Federal Government corporations are going at high yields with no aggravation about which are well-managed and which are not. But many private hospitals are not well-managed today. A fair number of them are in difficulty because of a gap between the timing of rate adjustments by Medicare and Medicaid and the continual rise in costs hospitals are having to meet. At any rate, hospitals able to stay in the black and within Government regulations are becoming the exception, rather than the rule.

By way of a parting caveat, remember Four Seasons—the nursing home that followed Penn Central onto the casualty list despite its growth prospects.

Q. I am in a 50 percent tax bracket. My mother is an invalid, and I need to get as high an income as I can to take care of her medical bills. My brother has advised me to buy the tax-exempt bonds of the State of Connecticut, but they yield only something like 7 percent. Would I not solve my problem more economically by buying the higher-yield utility bonds you have been recommending?

Miss N. A. B. (Norfolk, Connecticut)

A. Your brother is right. The 9 percent utility bonds look better at first glance, but you will have to pay Federal income tax on the interest you receive. In your 50 percent bracket the 9 percent on the taxable bonds is really only 4½ percent after taxes.

The appropriate comparison between tax-exempt and taxable yields is to figure out how much you would have to receive pre-tax to equal a tax-exempt rate. In your case those 7 percent Connecticut bonds give you an after-tax rate equivalent to a 14 percent yield on a pre-tax basis.

Q. What are utility bonds? How do you purchase them? How much is required to start with? How often do they pay interest?

Mrs. R. B. (Riverview, Michigan)

A. All utility companies finance their construction programs by selling bonds to the public. These bonds are mortgages on powerhouses, transmission lines, and the other obvious assets of utility companies. Anyone can buy them through any investment broker. If you don't know one, ask your bank to suggest one. These bonds sell in $1,000 denominations, and normally pay interest on a semiannual basis.

Pay no attention if the salesman advises you that stocks, not bonds, are the securities to buy in time of inflation. Brokers prefer to sell stocks rather than bonds—especially to small investors—because the commission on bonds is much less than that on stocks.

Q. I am 25 years old, single, have a good job and a promising future. A securities dealer has offered me the following investment plan: I give the investment company $10,000, which is used to purchase $100,000 in U.S. Treasury bills, margining the $90,000 difference, until prices go low enough to purchase long-term Government bonds. I'd like to make a lot of money before I take on the responsibility of a wife and family—but this sounds too good to be true.

Mr. J. D. (La Jolla, California)

A. It's bad enough to be true. The old saying about a fool and his money goes for anyone greedy enough to be borrowing to gamble on the timing of a bond market's recovery. With a market vulnerable to panic as the result of banks panicking for lack of lending power, 1970 has been the very worst time to borrow to carry securities of any kind. Borrowing on securities is for professionals able to count their mistakes and to take their losses, with enough cash on deposit in banks to make sure their loans won't be called.

Q. My husband is an invalid and unable to work. We are both in our late fifties. His pension is $125 a month, and my monthly salary is $350. Our entire savings of $15,000 is invested in a mutual fund. Although the dividends amount to $900 a year, I am getting panicky with the market situation. Is it advisable to sell the fund and buy bonds?

Mrs. R. B. (Columbus, Ohio)

A. Absolutely. Since you are in a low tax bracket, there is no need to accept the lower yield offered by tax-exempts. Why not buy any quality bond yielding 9 to 10 percent? Interest rates at such levels relieve you amateurs of the problem of selectivity.

Q. In your writings you often refer to the "E-bond swindle." Could you explain exactly what you mean by this?

Mr. S. L. (Bismarck, North Dakota)

A. Savings bond owners are paid an interest rate inequitably low relative to what money is worth today. Also, they are obliged to forgo the use of their interest when inflation has put a premium on cash. Over the years, savings bonds have been sold on the tricky suggestion that because the income is deferred, the tax on it is, too, and therefore presumably the savings bond holder is getting a tax advantage.

In fact, the savings bond holder is being shortchanged by the Government on taxes as well as on interest. The interest is paid on maturity or liquidation in the form of gain, but the savings bond holder who has meanwhile not had the use of the yield on his investment is obliged to pay tax on it as "ordinary income" instead of qualifying for the lower capital gains rate. The Government does not try to bilk the hard-nosed professional buyers of its bonds, certificates, and bills as it does the patriotic amateurs whom it has stuck with its savings bonds. It knows it must pay the going market rate to the pros, and it does.

Adding insult to injury, E-bond savers live in a fools' paradise while they save and then suffer a rude awakening when they cash in their bonds. In view of the fact that affluence has netted everybody much higher incomes (and put them into higher tax brackets!) than when the E-bonds now maturing were bought, the Treasury is getting a double windfall, chiseling on the interest rate it pays and cleaning up on the tax rate it collects. For a long time E-bond interest rates averaged out at only 3¾ percent a year, not payable in cash, while Treasury bills yielded over 6 or even over 7 percent, and U.S. Government agency bonds yielded over 8 percent, payable in cash by the day. Recognizing this the Government has recently raised the rate on bonds held to maturity from 5 percent to 5½ percent.

Q. I am one of the suckers whom you have described as caught in the E-bond swindle. I have $12,000 in E-bonds and want to dispose of them, but my bank's trust officer has advised me not to cash them in all at once, but to cash *in $1,000 a year and put that into a time deposit. Do you agree?*

Mr. L. T. (Birmingham, Alabama)

A. No. The reason given for not cashing in your E-bonds emphasizes what a bad investment they are and how unfairly the Government has been treating their owners. Even though the E-bond holder forgoes cash interest income and waits to take his return as gain, this gain is singled out for inequitable taxation as "ordinary income" instead of qualifying for a tax at the lower capital gains rates. If you wait to get rid of this bad investment, you will be speculating—first, that tax rates will not go up as a consequence of this inflation which has put everything else up, and secondly, that your own income will not go up, putting you in a higher tax bracket.

After you have read Chapter IX on advisors and how to choose them, you will do well to ponder the question whether bank trust officers may not run lawyers a close second for impracticality.

Q. My brother and I recently inherited from our father a sizable amount of money-good preferred stocks. I am a maiden lady past fifty, have never worked, and know nothing about the stock market. My brother says our stocks are going bad in the bear market and we should sell and put our money in convertible bonds, which won't go down as fast as stocks. Is this a good idea?

Miss O. T. (Rutland, Vermont)

A. Your brother is half-right. His sense of direction is correct, but he has chosen the wrong road map. Convertibles go up more than common stocks in good markets, which means that they go down more in bad markets. Any comparison between money-good preferreds and convertibles wants to take into account the income penalty the convertible buyer accepts in return for the presumption of a bigger play. Convertibles yield less than money-good senior securities—on the presumption that convertible bond owners will make up on gains what they will lose on income.

Q. I am 15 years old, a sophomore in high school and a serious student of the market. Since I was 12, I have been reading the financial news so that I now have considerable knowledge. From your columns, I gather that you do not consider convertible bonds the "ideal investment" that some other writers do. Would you explain why not?

Mr. A. L. S., Jr. (Chicago, Illinois)

A. With your "considerable knowledge" I am sure you are aware that *sophomore* means, literally, "wise fool." Knowledge needs to be tempered with judgment, usually an attribute of maturity.

At the bottom of sold-out bear markets, convertibles offer the best of both worlds because their value as bonds is on the verge of turning up, while the buyer need pay no premium for their "double-duty" or "fringe-benefit" value as stock options. But when convertibles can't be bought for their value as bonds—as they can't when their interest yields are uncompetitively low—they are really speculative trading media for sophisticated professionals only. So long as they can be bought for only nominal premiums above their current value as bonds, they are for plays for gain: the idea is that, as the stocks into which they offer options to convert rise in price, the value of the cheap stock option represented by the convertible will rise in value, too—the option grows more valuable as the stock rises (that is, if it does).

Opportunities to earn high income on convertibles are very rare indeed. Unlike property investment, it is unrealistic to expect them to enjoy steady long-term appreciation. They're for gains players, not for income investors. Gains players need judgment and experience, as well as knowledge. Speculators need a sense of timing.

Q. I have never noticed a recommendation of yours in favor of preferred stocks. It seems to me that they incorporate the best of both worlds, or do you disagree?

Mr. B. K. A. (Denver, Colorado)

A. I do. Because I believe that, certainly under present conditions, preferred stocks will freeze their holders into the worst of both worlds. If things go well, the preferred stockholder is the one class of stockholder left at the post. If things go poorly, he is too far down on the totem pole to protect himself as the bondholder can.

As a fixed-income security, preferred stocks are not yielding richer rates than bonds; and the next time money rates fall and fixed interest rates rise, they are not likely to go up as fast as bond prices. Altogether I see no incentive to buy preferreds—certainly short of a return to the 1930s (which I don't anticipate) when quality preferreds were going begging with accruals of big dividends waiting to be paid off. At any rate, this memory is a reminder that the only time preferreds are attractive is after a protracted speculative holocaust when arrears of cumulative dividends have built up.

Q. My wife and I are in our late seventies and hold various issues of municipal bonds. Aside from Social Security, these are our only source of income. There has been much discussion lately that Congress may change the tax-exempt status of municipal bonds. Does Congress have the power to alter the tax-exempt status of bonds already outstanding?

Mr. F. P. L. (St. Louis, Missouri)

A. Although Congress does have the power to do just about anything it pleases, I do not think it likely that it will outlaw tax exemption on either outstanding bonds or new issues. Such a vote would manufacture thousands of court cases on grounds of breach of faith with investors or nullification of Constitutional guarantees, but I do not believe that this concern will be the effective restraining factor.

The House and the Treasury were both influenced at the onset by the theory that, if municipal bonds became taxable, foundations, pension funds, and universities would take up the slack left by upper-bracket taxpayers and commercial banks, who are the big buyers today. But the harsh reality of the 1969 credit crisis sent this theory the way of all wishfulness. The selling of tax-exempt municipal bonds to upper-bracket taxpayers and commercial banks is the only way governors and mayors and county commissioners can finance state and local governments. Congressmen and Senators represent them in Washington.

Congress could achieve the same objective by passing the so-called "minimum income tax," requiring all upper-bracket recipients of tax-sheltered income from whatever source to pay some tax.

Q. What was the significance of A.T.&T.'s $1.5 billion financing in early 1970?

Mr. W. A. C. (St. Petersburg, Florida)

A. The offer by American Telephone and Telegraph Company to give its stockholders the opportunity to buy $1.5 billion of bonds with an equity kicker was one of the most important investment events of recent years—for a variety of reasons, each of them critically important in its own role, all of them interrelated, and none of them promising to undo the damage that has been done to the securities markets.

In the first place, "Ma Bell" made history by the size of this offer. It would be huge even as an exercise in United States Government finance. Not only is it unprecedented by any conventional standard of corporate funding; it measures the fantastic scale on which the American economy is continuing to manufacture what the economists call "effective demand"—that is, money-good demand for facilities.

The meaning for the economy of this bold move by A.T.&T. is clear and simple. The American economy is in no danger whatever of running out of work to do—as was widely feared by influential opinion as recently as the post-Korean War period. Its admitted troubles are centered not on the demand side of the fundamental marketplace divide, but on the supply side—in the demand for money. Answer the question everybody with any sense is asking—"Where is the money coming from to do everything plainly needing to be done?"—and every other economic question comes into clear focus.

The answer the Telephone Company has come up with points to the second reason why its money-raising operation is of such commanding importance in the investment history of 1970. Its approach is realistic enough to recognize that the crisis of illiquidity convulsing the investment markets is due not to a lack of overall liquidity, but rather to the mal-distribution of a very high level of liquidity.

Cash has run out of sight, and credit is being used up at the top of the financial pyramid. But in the popular income brackets—among modest savers, especially in smaller communities—money is still easy and ready to go to work if paid. A.T.&T. is aiming to look for it where it is, and to pay it what it requires. After all, no less than two-thirds of Telephone's vast army of stockholders own 100 shares or less, and this is the only mass market in which money can be raised on the scale required in America's democratic capitalism.

Hence "Ma Bell's" progressive strategy of marketing the $1.5 billion in $100 lots, instead of the conventional $1,000 denomination.

Q. Our immediate friends and neighbors have many interests in common—but none that we talk about more right now than our telephone stock. All of us seem to have it, and certainly all of us are worried about it. While it seems that all of our group have been relatively casual

*about selling other stocks from time to time, somehow we
have regarded our telephone stock as more than a commitment of money to a mere certificate, but, in addition, as
built into our way of life. Do you think that we should
stick it out, or do you regard the change in the times as
so drastic that you would recommend that we sell it?*

Mrs. J. F. S. (Scottsdale, Arizona)

A. I am well aware that telephone stock means more
than a mere investment to a representative cross-section
of America. Nevertheless, I strongly believe that it is the
better part of business prudence to sell the stock. I want
to be unmistakably clear that, in recommending the sale
of telephone stock, I am in no way casting a vote of no
confidence in this great company itself (I cannot repeat
often or emphatically enough the axiom that the top
standing of a company provides no insurance against its
stock going down in price).

In fact, the use to which I suggest putting the proceeds
of the sale of telephone casts a vote of confidence in the
company. For the simplest, smartest, safest thing to do
with the money is simply to switch it into telephone's
8¾ percent bond issue brought out early in 1970. Telephone stockholders making this switch will double their
income while limiting their risk and actually upgrading
the quality of their investment.

Because telephone bonds are as readily salable as telephone stocks, when the signals change and the all-clear
flashes again for quality stocks, the same switch can be
executed in reverse. When that happy day comes, bonds
will be selling at a lower yield, so that anyone selling tele-

phone at 8¾ percent then will be adding a profit to the high income earned in the meantime.

Q. What are index-linked bonds?

Mrs. E. J. A. (Irvington-on-Hudson, New York)

A. They are bonds linked to the cost-of-living index. The purpose of these bonds is to give money the same adjustment deal for renting itself out for interest that labor gets for hiring itself out for wages. For some years it has been standard operating practice in America for annual pay increases written in labor contracts to be supplemented as fast as the cost-of-living index rose. The idea has been to guarantee union members their pay increases in constant dollars. The practice of giving bondholders the same guarantee—of earning their interest in constant dollars—originated in Europe.

The most conspicuous illustration of this new trend was provided in June, 1970, when the great Netherlands-based, multi-national Phillips Lamp Corporation sold $250 million of bonds in the Euromarket on an index-linked basis.

A big switch is involved in the new practice, and it confirms my working premise that the old textbooks have become hopelessly out-of-date and impractical. They teach that money balks at buying bonds in time of inflation for fear of being paid back in depreciated currency. But the new institution of cost-of-living index-linked bonds is designed to insure the bondholder against this risk. Holders of index-linked bonds are invited to oblige their debtors to load the annual rate of inflation onto the going rate of interest at the time of issuance. The effect of this switch is to turn bondholders from victims of inflation—resisting it—into beneficiaries of inflation—going along with it.

A small trick is also built into this new device of the index-linked bond—the official cost-of-living index has been uniformly understating the rate of inflation. This means that buyers of index-linked bonds, although guaranteed the right to keep up with the Joneses, will not be doing as well as the profiteers from inflation—notably the service-labor trades. Despite the probability that the real cost of living will rise faster than statistical judgments ostensibly keeping pace with it, I expect the practice to grow in America as well as in Europe. And despite the likelihood that the cost of living and of doing business will rise faster than index-linked upward adjustments in supplemental interest payments, I have no doubt that new bond issues will continue to break all records.

Q. Some time ago you said, "It will take a bull market in bonds, paced by falling interest rates, to make the stock market safe again." How can one tell when there is a bull market in bonds? How is it indicated in the newspaper?

Mrs. G. K. (Wilmette, Illinois)

A. When Government agencies and big-name companies again begin to market their new bond issues at lower interest rates. If, for example, you read in the paper that new long-term issues are coming out at less than 7 percent, you will know that a big bull market in bonds is on. But be clear that the next bull market in bonds won't necessarily guarantee another bull market in stocks. Falling interest rates will merely begin to reduce the large risks now overhanging the stock market.

CHAPTER IX

Advisors

FREE advice is worth exactly what it costs. That is the beginning of wisdom for would-be investors, ready to make the plunge and looking around for counsel as to where, when, and for how much. Another phrase to remember is the famous "He who is his own lawyer has a fool for a client"—it applies to "do-it-yourself" investment, as well. Both these rules boil down to the fact that most amateur investors need professional advice and must pay the going premium that proven professionals command.

The immediate trouble is that one of the great social costs of inflation has been to raise this premium above what many investors can afford. Time was when, given the going rate of a half of one percent for investment advisory fees, anyone with capital of $100,000 could afford to buy, and count on getting, competent investment advice.

Today more people than ever have investment availability of between $20,000 and $100,000, but they can't afford the cost of paid advice. And in our complex world the price of advice is pushed even higher by the ever-increasing need for the specialist. Many of the people who can barely afford to hire one advisor really need a battery of them to get the best advice.

This increasing cost has helped make mutual funds attractive for the small investor, since professional money management is part of the deal. Others get round the problem by buying bonds—if they can afford to put them away and forget about them—or property. One of the many differences between property and other investments is that it is almost impossible to buy a house or land without professional and professionally paid advice. But $100,000 will buy you a good deal of property and buy management with it—you can't say the same for securities.

Among those who want to stay in the securities markets there are always the ones who fall back on the opportunistic expedient of trying to get investment advice on the cheap from lawyers and accountants. To pay higher legal fees and higher accountants' fees and get no investment advice would be a real bargain. Lawyers and accountants notoriously run second only to teachers, preachers, doctors, and retired military men as unsuccessful investors and impractical businessmen.

This points out another rule in seeking and accepting investment advice. Ask the person giving it how well he has done in translating his own income into capital. The next question to ask is "What are you going to make from me?" If he says he's not going to make anything, watch out! Don't think the advice you get from me is free. The newspapers that buy my columns pay me, and you pay them. You are also paying me by buying this book.

Always be sure when making arrangements with professional advisors—whether banks, trust companies, mutual funds, insurance firms, investment brokers, accountants, lawyers, or property managers—that you get straight exactly what the deal is beforehand. Find out what they expect to make, and on what basis, and whether they will make something whether their clients do well or not. If they say they can't make more than a certain amount out of you, they could be very good or very bad.

And be suspicious if advisors do not ask *you* questions. A good investment advisor should want to know all about your circumstances, your medical expenses, dependents, your retirement plans, above all, how much you can afford to lose or to tie up, and how quick or big a return you need. The advisor who does not inquire searchingly into all these factors, and more, wants only his fee—all of them want that, but the ones who do well are the ones who want their fees to grow with your money.

A final word about "do-it-yourself" investment. The number of people capable of managing their own money in the investment markets is small. Possibly it does everybody some good to lose some money in an effort to decide what they want to do with it. Anyone's ability to choose an advisor with prudence and practicality depends on his ability to make a clear identification of his investment aims.

Q. I am a college senior due to graduate and receive an Air Force commission in December. My wife and I have $465 in S & L accounts and add $180 per month to them from our salaries. We own 150 shares in a Springfield investment company and have $225 invested in a mutual fund. We also have about $500 on deposit with a St. Louis *credit union accumulated through weekly withdrawals from my pay.*

We would like to take this money and start investing in the stock market. Do you feel we have enough money to begin with? Since I do not know what plans the Air Force has for me, would it be wise to use a large brokerage house and communicate by mail, or go to a local broker whom I know? What do you think of giving a trusted broker power of attorney and letting him "play" with the money? Should we continue to add $25 a month to the mutual fund?

Mr. W. R. T. (Carbondale, Illinois)

A. Looks to me like up to this point you have been getting as much out of your education as I am confident the country will get out of it during the years to come.

It's never too soon to begin investing, and no amount is too small. But make sure your investment operation begins only as an addition to the savings reserve you decide is irreducible as a practical constant under your circumstances. Once this is decided, extra cash you accumulate can be used for investment.

So long as you remain where you are, I think that it would make sense to work with your local broker. You don't have enough money for it to be worth his while to "take" you if he's not on the level. But the fact that he is a personal acquaintance should not blind you to the wisdom of keeping score on his recommendations and developing your own judgment of his judgments.

Wait until the Air Force reassigns you before crossing the next bridge. Big brokerage firms are no better than their local offices, which necessarily vary from city to city.

I don't think much of the idea of trusting a broker with power of attorney and letting him play with your money. You don't have enough money or experience to speculate. You'll do well to make your wife a partner in your investment operation.

I think that you would be wise to continue adding $25 a month to your mutual fund account and to let the dividends accumulate. Learn to read its regular reports and see if your broker's recommendations can match its record over a period of time.

Q. I am 44 years old and have a wife, an 18-year-old son, and a 14-year-old daughter. At present, we have adequate savings for a cash reserve and for college education funds for the children, and would like to begin investing about $100 a month in the stock market. However, I have neither the time nor the interest to become as acquainted with the market as I should be in order to invest wisely without outside help. My intent during the last few years was to invest between $300 and $500 every three months, which would provide continuous periodic investing with reasonably low brokers' fees. However, I did not take the time to follow through with this plan. Any suggestions which you may have for our investment program will be appreciated.

Mr. B. O. W. (Allen Park, Michigan)

A. Your problem isn't what to do with your money, but what to do with your time. It is unrealistic to expect your money to work any harder for you than, by your own admission, you are willing to work to learn how to use your money. If you won't take the time to follow

through on learning how to handle your money, then you
have to pay the going price for someone to handle it
for you.

*Q. I am 55 years of age and never went to college. I
have no skill and never earned more than $130 a week.
Whenever I've invested in real estate or stocks, I've given
them the kiss of death.*

*I own 435 shares of a leading auto parts stock. I also
have 2,000 shares of another $3.50 stock which I bought
last April at $4.25 on a tip from one of my successful
friends. It was supposed to hit 13 in six weeks. This has
been my first and last "tip." I'm going to sell this stock
this week.*

Mr. A. S. (Highland Park, Illinois)

A. You strike me as having earned your "R" for realist.
But you won't change your luck so long as you go on
taking tips on junk. Perhaps your "friend" is successful
because he gives tips like this one instead of acting on them
himself. Charge up your loss to the cost of experience.

*Q. We always seem to do the wrong thing. We sold
Sperry Rand at $23, just when it was going up, simply
because we had got tired of watching it not get anywhere.
We also sold Hammond Organ, but we should have sold
it years ago, just after it split and went up again to almost
$50. We now hold 800 shares of a stock purchased at
around $4. It went up to $9 right after we bought but,
again, we didn't sell. Then it dropped to as low as $1.50.
Within the last six months, it has been going up: the other*

*day it went to over $10. What should we do? We have
already had several opinions—all different.*

Mrs. A. J. S. (Elgin, Illinois)

A. Three strikes are out. This game isn't for you. You
are the typical "set-up-to-lose" market player who belongs
in mutual funds.

Take the pledge and turn your back on stock tips,
market-playing, and free advice. Inveterate tip-takers
need an organization to get them off stocks in the same
way Alcoholics Anonymous straightens out boozers.

*Q. I have inherited about $100,000 worth of stocks.
As I know nothing about stocks, I have a trust agreement
with a bank to manage them for me. They charge one-
half of one percent for this service. Should I continue this
arrangement?*

Mrs. J. S. W. (Butte, Montana)

A. By your own account, you need a shepherd. Your
bank is charging you the standard, going, professional
rate for investment advice. Ask not how much your trust
advisor is charging you, but how prudent and profitable
his advice is. Ask also whether an institution can pay a
competent staff after billing you a mere $500 a year and
still make out. Your apparent bargain may be its disaster
and yours.

*Q. Would you please tell us how to find someone to
contact about our investments whom we can trust?*

Mr. W. J. H. (Fort Lauderdale, Florida)

A. Talk to your local commercial banker and ask to be put in touch with two or three broker-dealers whom the bank trusts to handle most of its investment department business. Ask if it uses advisors operating a mutual fund.

Q. *Mine is the familiar story of a widow seeking advice and not knowing to whom to turn. No two brokers seem to agree. I am 57, employed at $75 a week, and the sole support of myself and my son, who hopes to finish college in two years. My $25,000 home is paid for. I have $10,000 in savings and manage to live on my salary plus dividends. I have common stocks worth $66,000 and $13,000 in a growth fund. I am told my income would be enhanced if I were to convert all my stocks to a mutual fund, but I am not convinced of the logic of such a move. However, I am not qualified to handle my own portfolio. What do you advise?*

Mrs. L. S. B. (*Boca Raton, Florida*)

A. Your judgment is every bit as sound as your budgeting. The more brokers you consult, the more conflicting recommendations you can expect. Several competitive mutual funds, each emphasizing a different objective, are the answer for you. Increased income plus long-term gain could then become your objective. A considerable portion of your savings, too, will bear switching into funds.

Q. *What is your opinion on investment managing firms? Where can one check on their performance? One firm claims a 34 percent return average and accepts accounts only of $10,000 and up. We have just $10,000 to* *invest. Would subscribing to such a service be wise? We would like to plan now for my husband's retirement in ten years. He makes $15,000 a year and has a substantial amount in his company retirement fund. We have three children nearly ready for college, and we have money set aside for their education. Also, we have $6,000 in a mutual fund and a trust fund of $6,000. What do you advise?*

Mrs. R. E. T. (Spokane, Washington)

A.   Counseling firms observe a high standard of ethics, but the only public check on their performance is offered by those that operate mutual funds, as a number of prominent ones do. Check the credentials and client references of any firm offering to accept accounts as small as $10,000 for individual supervision. The bare minimum for most is $100,000. I'd also be very dubious of any claim suggesting that a 34 percent annual return could be par for the course.

Mutual funds literally mutualize investment advice for people unable to afford to hire their own. I think your best bet is to put the $10,000 in a fund. Check your present fund's performance before deciding whether to add to it or to diversify.

Q.   Why do brokers so often disagree on stocks? Some time ago, I bought 60 shares of an airline stock at my broker's suggestion. He then went on vacation. Every day since, the stock has gone down. I just talked to my broker's substitute, and he told me that airlines have had their day, and that if I had asked his advice he would not have suggested this stock. I can't help feeling that any old stocks

*are sold to women because it's assumed they don't know
any better.*

Miss L. N. (Gary, Indiana)

A. As the saying goes, such disagreements are what
make horse races—and markets. In the case of your particular speculative mishap—and that is what it was, because
your letter doesn't make you out to be a real investor—
I see no reason to suspect that your broker was doing anything but following the popular parade into airlines while
the pros were bailing out.

Your broker's substitute is better informed than your
broker. Stocks that have been institutional investor favorites take it on the chin when they fall out of fashion with
the big holders. The smart game for the little fellow is
to wait until after institutional selling has done its damage and recreated investment values.

*Q. My sister is a widow with two children, aged 22
and 20. She works at a civil service job. The son is draft-
exempt and is working, but contributes nothing to his
mother at this point. The daughter intends to finish
college.*

*My sister's favorite comment is: "The broker says to
buy stock, the real estate salesman says to buy real estate,
the bank says to leave your money in savings." She has
at present about $20,000 in savings accounts, another
$6,000 in utility stocks and bonds, and $6,000 in a mutual
fund. She is inclined to buy more stock, but I feel that
mutual funds would be best. Your comments would be
helpful.*

Mr. H. W. W. (Wheaton, Illinois)

A. Does your sister believe that you are selling mutual funds on the side? I think you're giving her good, objective advice.

If her son is living at home, it certainly is in order for him to be making a contribution to her household.

Q. Do you consider it advisable to invest in Mexico under supervision of an investment counseling firm that is registered with the SEC in the United States? If so, is the present student unrest in Mexico such that investment should be deferred?

Mr. J. W. B. (Emporia, Kansas)

A. For an investment counselor to be registered with the SEC provides no guarantee against advice that may lose money for you. SEC supervision provides legal protection against investment advisory and securities merchandising practices that have been outlawed, not an assurance of profit income or return of capital.

If student unrest or civil disorder were an investment factor, no investments in this country would be safe—as, clearly, many are. The most compelling argument, in my judgment, against investment in Mexico is that if money could not be prudently and profitably put to work in the United States, it will not be safe anywhere else. Consequently, I think that you'll do just as well and take less risk by keeping your money at work in this country.

Q. When my husband died I had $63,000 to invest. A brokerage firm was recommended to me and I trusted it. The salesman bought unwisely—he bought and sold, always telling me it would increase my income—until I *have nearly nothing left now. I have learned since that he had no license to sell in Florida. Of course, after I found out what he was doing, I did not let him sell any more, but he had wasted so much. Is there anything I can do?*

Mrs. H. A. N. (*Pompano Beach, Florida*)

A. Your plight recalls the question in vogue at the time of the 1929 crash. On being shown the brokers' yachts at anchor off Palm Beach, an investment innocent who had been taken asked, "But where are the customers' yachts?" Not even professionals can hope to beat the market by playing hopscotch from stock to stock. Anyone in your position who permits a stock salesman to churn in this fashion is bound to be fleeced by commission-hungry stock salesmen. Your best bet is to consult a lawyer and have him contact the firm that employed this salesman, with a view to exploring whether you may have a claim.

Q. *A few minutes after noon one day, my broker told me he did not have a buyer for the 200 shares of stock I had ordered sold earlier. Between that time and exchange closing, the stock went up $3, but I received the lowest price. Can I find out the time the stock went up?*

Mrs. D. J. D. (*Chicago, Illinois*)

A. Either your broker, whom I hope you are now in the process of firing, didn't give you the straight story, or you didn't get it straight, but the way the market works is not as the result of brokers with sell orders looking for buyers. Your particular stock is listed on the New York Stock Exchange. The N.Y.S.E. keeps track of the time of each transaction in its listed securities. Check your records and your recollection and write to their complaint department. They can give you a complete rundown.

Q. I have a considerable investment in negotiable bonds now being held by a New York brokerage firm for safekeeping. The firm sends me the interest as it comes due; there is no charge for this service, and it is a great convenience. My local broker tells me the bonds are insured fully. You have recommended that stocks similarly held by a broker be removed to a safe-deposit box. Do you think the bonds ought to be also?

Mrs. P. M. (Tulsa, Oklahoma)

A. I think you and your broker would be better off if you were to put your bonds in your safe-deposit box. Brokers have been caught in a very severe cost squeeze, and they have good reason to be careful and to get rid of responsibilities that hurt their overheads without helping their revenue.

Q. I have always left my certificates in "street name," and my attorney, accountant, and the trust department of my bank all agree that the safeguards required by the Securities and Exchange Commission are such that the practice is entirely safe. In what way do you differ from their views?

Mr. W. A. A. (Pompano Beach, Florida)

A. Contrary to your impression and the advice you have been receiving, all Wall Street was thrown into turmoil as the result of the difficulty stock buyers experienced in getting deliveries of their purchases, and stock sellers in getting their money. "Fails" is the term used to describe the delivery logjam, and it means exactly what it says. "Fails" are the reason the stock exchanges experimented with Wednesday closings and with 2 P.M. closings. The problem of making sound investment judgments is difficult enough—why compound it by inviting technical problems not of your own making and beyond your control? Investors unable to get delivery on their purchases have been losing untold income in uncollected dividends.

Q. Is this a good time to sell a $25,000 portfolio of blue-chip stocks and buy into a mutual fund? We have about $5,000 of capital gain. My broker says that now is the time, when prices are low. However, as common stocks lose value more rapidly than mutual fund shares, how can this be a profitable move when the sales charge is also considered? This is our only asset. We are seven years from retirement, with no pension except Social Security. What is your advice?

Mrs. G. W. (Deerfield Beach, Florida)

A. I think your broker is half-right—this is a very good time to take any $5,000 gain in blue chips. Put the proceeds into bonds, even though your broker may resist this because his cut on bond commissions will be next to nothing.

Q. Can I buy bonds through a stock broker?

Mr. C. G. (Seattle, Washington)

A. Any broker can help you buy bonds—but of course not all brokers are anxious to do so. Now that the investing public has shown itself prudent enough to take advantage en masse of the long-term bargain offered by record high yields, competition will decide the argument. Brokers who want to stay in business with customers having money to invest are getting the message and are servicing the demand for bonds.

Q. *You recently recommended "investments that are entirely tax-sheltered—like municipals maturing in one year." How does one find out about them and get hold of them?*

Mrs. A. M. B. (Newman Grove, Nebraska)

A. The interest paid on bonds that are sold by municipalities (like the one you live in) to finance the cost of building schools, hospitals, roads, and so on, is tax-free. Go to your local bank and ask the officer in charge of its investments to furnish a list of municipals due to be retired and repaid in one year.

Q. *In the near future we will get $135,000 from the sale of a property, and we have been told that in order to avoid taxes we would be well advised to put this cash into a living trust.*

Mr. F. W. (Palatine, Illinois)

A. I'm afraid that you have been ill-advised. If you have a gain on the property you are selling, you will owe a tax regardless of whether or not you put the money in trust. Consult an accountant on your tax problem. Investment questions often boil down to tax questions. An accountant can help you more than a broker can.

Q. I have followed your writings through the years with much interest. I would like advice regarding my son's investments. He lacks knowledge of investments and depends a great deal upon my advice. He has a wife and four children and is in a salary range of $30,000 a year. He could accumulate a sizable estate in the next 20 years with proper management—I know that a savings account is necessary, but one needs to invest otherwise in order to reach the highest goal. I feel that he should acquire the help of a good professional investment manager. What is the best way for him to proceed?

Mrs. E. S. H. (Joliet, Illinois)

A. You're giving him good advice. Be sure that you remind him to insure his wife and children against the risk that he may die leaving them unprovided for. Why don't you suggest that he ask the treasurer of his company for an introduction to the advisor to his pension or profit-sharing fund?

Q. In 1929 I began buying stock in the large corporation I worked for. Over the years I accumulated a few hundred shares of the stock, but I did not keep a record of the cost, as income tax was not a factor. Is there any way I can arrive at the cost so as to figure capital gains?

Mr. A. O. (Boca Raton, Florida)

A. I assume that you do have the stock certificates themselves. Make a list of the dates on these certificates and take it to the public library—or to a broker who is willing to help you—and look in the newspaper files to check what the stock was trading for on those dates.

Q. Is $160 a year too much to pay for a weekly newsletter on the business situation?

Mr. N. P. (Cedar Rapids, Iowa)

A. If you get one good money-saving or money-making idea a year out of your $160 subscription, it's a bargain.

Q. My bankers advised me not to buy Government agency bonds, saying they are not guaranteed in any way by the Federal Government. Please comment.

Mr. G. M. (Mount Carmel, Illinois)

A. Some Government bonds are guaranteed, and some aren't—and still others are in part. Bankers need lawyers themselves and, therefore, stray into deep water when they double in brass giving free legal or investment advice —which is worth what it costs. A lawyer will stand you in better stead than a banker on this question relating to fine print.

Q. My lawyer keeps telling me of "hot tips" in the stock market. Should I listen to him?

Mr. W. I. A. (Gary, Indiana)

A. Beware of investment advice or speculative leads from legal advisors. The lawyers who give the best legal advice long ago learned to stick to their own profession.

Q. For our son's 21st birthday we would like to give him a share of stock. We could invest approximately $100. What type of stock could you get for that amount, and where would we purchase it?

Mrs. G. R. R. (Wilmette, Illinois)

A. You'll make more sense as investment guides and as parents if you give the youngster the money and tell him to go out and celebrate.

CHAPTER X

Omens and Portents

WHAT Shall I Do With My Money? is a question normally easier to ask than to answer. It takes a money crisis to simplify the answer as well. Hang on to it. Don't expect risks you may take with it to reward you any faster than you have been able to reward yourself by accumulating your money in the first place.

Take the way you became a "thousandaire"—by putting aside a more or less regular portion of your earnings. After you did this for a while, you woke up to discover that you had graduated from being an earner and a saver into being an earner and an investor. Most people who have unhappy experiences as investors, or as speculators, make their own trouble by buying the illusion that unearned income can be trusted to compound faster than earned income.

What you want to do with your money is to use it to buy you the freedom to do what you want to do, not only with your money, but with your life—the freedom to choose. This means the freedom to work less, if that is what you want or need to do. It means the freedom to do

more things with your time for less money, if that is what
you want to do. And it means the freedom to do with your
money what you think makes sense, instead of being
forced or frightened to change your planning and your
budget just because the stock market happens to break,
the banks get tight for money, or medical costs rise. The
most sensible reason to want to be well off is to be not
only comfortable but free.

It takes a money crisis to teach people who worked,
and went without, and took chances to get money, how
free and easy they were with it while they still had it to
put to work. It takes a money crisis to demonstrate how
much those who need money will pay those who still have
it for the privilege of hiring it. There is nothing like a
money crisis to put those who have been hanging on to it
into the driver's seat.

Today's credit squeeze is without precedent—not
merely because those who need money and can get it
need to borrow unprecedentedly large sums and find
themselves obliged to pay unprecedentedly high prices
for it; and not merely because those unable to get it are
producing unprecedentedly bigger bankruptcies. What is
new and different about today's money squeeze is that
it is the first one in modern history to be presided over by
a Government which has persuaded itself and everyone
else that it could protect itself and everyone else against
running itself and everyone else out of money.

The late John Maynard Keynes was the prophet of the
new era that saw Government power take over as the
money power. His most influential assertion about money
was that the Government had "claimed the right not only
to enforce the dictionary, but also to write the dictionary."

Money was worth what the Government said it was worth, he insisted. The world accepted his teaching as an article of faith, and this faith worked. It produced money —mountains of it—and (especially with the coming of World War II) it put the money to work. The Keynesian formula remained trustworthy from the onset of the new era of big government, inaugurated by Franklin D. Roosevelt in 1933, until Lyndon Johnson handed on the bankruptcy over which he had found himself presiding to Richard Nixon in 1969. No government has ever been as big or as powerful as the American Government. No government has ever had more money or immobilized itself more for lack of so much of it.

The discovery that it was the biggest bankruptcy in history over which Johnson was presiding came from another discovery; namely, that what had started out to be the great money game had turned into another endlessly long, endlessly costly war game. And while government in America had irrefutably demonstrated that indeed it had the power Keynes said it had, and while it had also demonstrated that it knew how to use it to play the money game, it did not know how to use it to play the war game.

Theoretically, money is more than ever what the Government in Washington says it is. As a practical matter, however, the Government no longer knows what to say. And when the Government does not know what to say about money, it loses control over what it is doing.

Under the peculiar rules prescribed by the American Constitution with its two-headed sovereignty, the President as Commander-in-Chief can exercise the power to make any war he pleases, but he must persuade Congress to give him the money he needs to pay for both his military and his civilian operations.

War is so momentous that once a President asks Congress to declare it in the conventional way, he has an excuse for calling off every other game he is under pressure to play. But when a President wheels and deals himself a war game operated under the guise of a money game, he loses the option to call off business as usual.

A war that is not intelligible to the tax-paying public has no chance of becoming politically acceptable to the Congress. The President cannot explain, let alone enforce, the new rules demanded by his continuing war game either to the Congress, upon which he depends for his financing, or to the public, upon which he and the Congress depend for their tenure. He cannot impose them on the financial markets, which have come to depend on the Government for their stability and on whose stability in turn the Government has come to depend for its money. Once the Government shuttled itself out of the money game and shuffled itself into the war game, it found itself helpless to observe the basic rule of war, which any government ignores at its peril; namely, that the priority demands of war override the claims of the market and the convenience of money-users participating in the market. Measures taken to meet a military emergency call for supporting measures of economic emergency.

But the war, being unintelligible and unacceptable, has therefore proved unfinanceable. The President, instead of solving the problem, has denied it—by promising to end the war sooner rather than later. The fact is that whether this particular war game in Indochina ends quickly, or drags on, we are in a condition of financial emergency—

not only with the political-military emergency in the Middle East, but with the social emergency in the cities and the accelerating crisis in the pollution of our environment. These are rival claimants for the same kind of financing—as to amount and as to time—as a full-fledged military emergency. Moreover, the social and ecological emergencies demanding to be financed, but remaining unfinanced, command the public consensus validating their demands while the military operation actually being committed for does not.

The malady of inflation known as "all-at-once-itis"—inflation for guns and inflation for butter is another way of putting it—has been using up our savings just when the demand for savings to be drawn on to finance new borrowings is rising faster than ever. In spite of all the money the country has dispersed abroad and misspent at home, it still has a great deal—but not enough in concentrated enough lots to meet its borrowing needs; and it is spending more on its present way of living and has less to finance its future requirements than it can afford.

So long as the money game was on, and everyone who had or could get money was doing better than ever playing one or another part in it, money was looking for new places to go and new work to do, confident that frontier opening meant new investment and profit opportunities. But government, business, and Wall Street all ran out of money just when the way the game was played was reversed. As the distress of the big Federal Government borrower spread to just about every other government borrower throughout the country, and as the distress of the country's governments spread to the businesses from which they raise their money, money-raisers began to chase money-owners. So long as this chase is on, money will be better off letting itself be chased rather than chasing. And you will be better off hanging on to it and weighing the competing bids for it rather than being in a hurry to put it to work.

Because the money game has turned into a war game; and because the war game will be scored against America until the American Government figures a way to get itself out of the hole into which it has dug itself, another and more ominous judgment—seemingly unrelated to the world of money, but decisive in the politics of crisis in the 20th century—is asserting its anxious relevance upon the frightened new world of the 1970s.

It harks back to the echo of the shot that announced the onset of World War I in 1914. That echo still carries in the words of Lord Grey, Britain's philosopher-diplomat, who was then her Foreign Secretary. "The lights are going out all over Europe," he said. "They will not go on again in our time."

The lights can be made to go on again, in our time, and in a matter of a few years—which is not very much time as economic man's experience accumulates. But they will not go on again until the dual sovereignty of President and Congress responsible for managing America's war game and its money game resolve their differences and compromise their demands upon one another as the condition of reopening their negotiations with the outside world. Until they do, foreign policy trouble will keep on making money trouble, and America's cities and environment will continue to deteriorate.

Eventually the President, this one or the next, and Congress, this one or the next, will compose their differ-

ences and hang together—if only because the incentives
of political survival will confirm Ben Franklin's sage warning that the alternative is to hang separately.

The question "How soon is eventually" recalls the col-
loquial answer of the legendary Vermont farmer who,
when asked in the middle of an August drought by a visiting city tourist whether it would rain, replied, "Not right
away."

For money-users—small and large, private and corporate, economic and political—who have read this manual
and are resolved to learn how to use it, caution is clearly
the first order of the day. A rider to it duplicates the
muscular logic of the labor market: "No contract, no
work." The laborer being worthy of his hire, so money is
of its. In the labor market the sellers of skills are setting
the rates of wages. In the money markets the lenders of
credit are setting the rate of interest in exactly the same
way—not as a matter of right, but as a matter of power,
which is more persuasive.

When caution is the order of the day for money, it
behooves those who still have it to travel more warily
than even the proverbial Senator Soaper, who in his
heyday was said to be the only living animal able to run
—as he did constantly—with both ears to the ground at
once. I suggest that the way to do so now is by checking
each and every money-using decision by three rules of
thumb. I expect all three will remain pointed in the
direction of danger until all three together again signal
the all-clear.

The first rule of thumb is the political one. The signal
to watch requires no financial expertise whatsoever. It
takes nothing but a citizen-taxpayer's relatively casual

awareness of the Washington news. So long as the President and Congress continue to play their own private political war game, the money markets are going to continue being caught in the middle and to be hurt. The key point to remember is that the Congress cannot govern, but that the President cannot govern without the Congress. The next time of decision for the markets to mark off on the calendar is the next Presidential year.

The second is the financial one. It is centered in the bond market, on the long-term side of it, which is where the real cost of money is determined. The most sensitive and alarming evidence of distress suffered by the borrower having the greatest political strength—namely the United States Government—is that it has lost control over its own demand for money. The Federal Reserve system is the lender of last resort to distressed borrowers. The Treasury is becoming the borrower of last resort. Everybody from the housing industry to busted railroads is going to the Treasury to ask it to raise money on their behalf.

The more distress the Government spreads, the bigger the burden it places on the bond market, the more risks it piles on those who need money, and the richer the rewards it finds itself obliged to pay those prudent enough to hang on to their money until they are paid for putting it to work safely.

The key point to be remembered by everyone waiting for the all-clear to sound is that it cannot and will not until long-term interest rates come down. This cannot and will not happen, while the war game is on, until the Government does the necessary to bring them down. The *how* of this does not belong in this manual, but rather in the very different kind of book at which I am doing my best now.

One source of hope to note now is the stock market. Since today's borrowings are not likely to be repaid by a rise in earnings, the corporations that are survivors—as distinct from candidates for bankruptcy—have no alternative but to turn their eyes away from the over-burdened bond market to the stock market and to go to it for the permanent capital they will need in lieu of more borrowings and earnings.

Meanwhile, the third rule of thumb is the speculative one. And it is centered in the stock market, which is now the speculative arena for money-users who have not run out of money or who have not been paid to play in greener pastures. The key point to remember is that the stock market cannot and will not get back on an even keel until the bond market becomes buoyant again. A resilient bond market by no means guarantees a restabilized stock market, but a positively rejuvenated bond market is the precondition for a stabilized stock market.

The *when* of this is best answered in terms of the where —more precisely, the not-where. The one place the present distress of the stock market is certain not to end is on the front page of the newspapers or on the top spot of the nightly television newscast. What the stock market needs before it can come alive and be jumping again is a long, big sleep.

When it wakes up, it will look back on the last trip it took into get-rich-quick land as an hallucination. The big secret about Wall Street is that while there is a quick way to lose money, there are no quick ways to make it there nor, indeed, anywhere else. Money-making is for those who have saved enough of it to have it to put to work for them. Not only is time money, it takes time to make money.

Index

accountants, 188
advisors, 174–176, 183–184, 190–191
  "do-it-yourself" vs. professional advice, 174, 176, 179–180
  fees, 95–97, 104–105, 174–175, 180
  types of:
    accountants, 175, 188
    banks, 164–165, 180–181, 190
    brokers, 50–51, 157–158, 176–179, 181–188
    investment counseling firms, 181–184
    investment managing firms, 184
    lawyers, 175, 190
    mutual fund management, 87–88, 92, 95–96, 100–102, 175
American Stock Exchange, 124
amortization, 65–66, 71
annuities, 28–29, 36. *See also* insurance
A.T.&T., 50, 169–170

banks:
  advisors, 164–165, 180–181, 190
  credit cards, 55–58
  effects of liquidity crisis on, 51–52, 135–136
  stocks, 134–136
  See also certificates of deposit, checking accounts, savings accounts
beneficiary (of insurance), 27, 39
blue chip stocks, 121–122, 126–127, 187
  See also stocks
bonds, 148–150
  as investment, 151–152, 162–163, 167, 187–188
  high-yield, 131–132
  low-risk, 53–54
  short-term vs. long-term, 155
  types of:
    bankrupt corporations, 154–155
    convertible debentures, 150–151, 165–167

bonds (*cont.*)
  types of (*cont.*)
    corporate (utility), 50, 148,
      161–162, 169–171
    E-Bonds, 32–33, 148–149,
      163–165
    Government agency, 148–
      149, 157–158, 164, 190
    hospital, 160–161
    index-linked, 172–173
    municipals, 148–149, 168,
      188
    Treasury, 148–149, 155–
      158
  interest rates, 148–151
    "call protection," 148
    ceilings, 148–149, 157–158
  issuers, 148–149
  price:
    deep discounts, 150, 153–
      154
    discounts, 153
    premiums, 153
  ratings, 158–160
  yields, 150, 153
  taxable vs. tax exempts, 117,
    150, 161, 163, 168, 188
  See also bond market
bond market, 147, 149, 152,
  162–163, 173, 198–201.
  See also bonds
brokers, 50–51, 157–158, 176–
  179, 181–188
  "fails," 186–187
  fees, 151, 161–162, 187–188
  "put and call" broker, 116
  use of large vs. small broker-
    age, 176–178
budgets:
  budgeting for:
    cash reserve, 23, 32–34

    housing, 30–31, 78–79
    insurance (life), 24–25,
      35–38, 40–41
    investment, 29–30, 33–34,
      37–38
    medical costs, 22–23, 30–
      31, 35–36, 39–40, 53–54
    rents, 23, 31–32
    taxes, 23, 30–33
  planning family budget, 21–
    24, 30–31, 40–42, 192

cash:
  demand for, 44
  types of, 43
  use of, 45
  See also checking accounts,
    cash equivalents
cash equivalents, 43–44
  types of:
    certificates of deposit, 50–
      51
    commercial paper, 51–52
    credit cards, 55–58
    savings deposits, 44, 47–48
    time deposits, 50–51
    Treasury bills, 49–51, 155–
      156, 164
cash reserve:
  accumulation of, 22–23, 30,
    33–34, 45–46, 79–80
  reasons for, 32–33, 47–48
  use of, 52–53, 73–74, 89–90,
    177
certificates:
  savings, 95
  stock, 186–187, 189–190
  trustee, 154
certificates of deposit, 50–51
checking accounts, 46–47
  use of, 38, 43–44

Church of England, 59–60
commercial paper, 44, 51–52
condominiums, 65
conglomerates, 139. *See also* stocks
cost of living:
  increases in, 21–23, 41
  index-linked bonds, 172–173
  providing for increases, 23–24, 30, 32–33
credit, 55–57
  line of, 46
credit cards:
  bank credit cards, 55–58
  dangers of, 57–58
  interest on, 43–44, 57–58
  special uses of, 56–58
credit ratings, 55–56
cyclical stocks, 122–123, 140–141. *See also* stocks

deflation:
  in economy, 1929–1933, 15
  in stock market, 12–13
Depression, 14–16
dividends:
  mutual funds, 91–92, 99
  stocks:
    non-taxable, 131
    yield spread, 108–111, 123, 130
Dow-Jones industrial average, 121

endowment, 28. *See also* insurance

Federal Reserve Board, 13, 136
Franklin, Benjamin, 198

gold:
  buying of, 143
  pricing of, 115

gold stocks, 143
Gould, Edson, 111
Grey, Lord, 197
growth (glamour) stocks, 121–122, 126–130. *See also* stocks

homes:
  budget for, 30–31, 78–79
  condominium, 65
  See also mortgages, property, rents

I.B.M., 127–129
inflation:
  effects of:
    on bond yields, 150, 152, 155–156, 172–173
    on business, 18–20, 136–137, 140–141
    on cost of living, 22–23, 32–33, 174
    on mortgage market, 85–86
    on rents, 23, 31–32, 159–160
    on stock market, 12–13, 18–20, 45, 94, 109, 111, 113, 115, 129–131
  general diagnosis of, 18–20, 193–197
  protection against, 45–46, 56–57
  through insurance, 24, 27
  through mortgages, 61, 67–69, 71–72, 74–75
  through property investment, 60–61, 80–81, 83
  through savings accounts, 47–48
  solutions to, 197–201

installment purchasing, 31
insurance, 24–29, 35–42
  premiums, 24, 26–29
  purchasing guidelines, 24–25,
    29, 35–38, 102–103
  for self-employed, 39–40
  taxes on, 39
  types of:
  annuities (life), 28–29, 36
  medical, 35–36, 39–40
  permanent life, 26–28
  term insurance (life), 25–27
interest rates, 44–45
  on bonds, 54, 148–151, 156–
    158, 163–164
  on cash equivalents, 44
    certificates of deposit, 50–
      51
    commercial paper, 52
    credit cards (bank), 55–
      58
    savings deposits, 47–48
    Treasury bills, 49, 164
  on money stocks, 123, 134–
    137
  on mortgages, 63, 66–68, 74–
    75
  effects on:
    bond market, 147–154,
      167, 173
    money market, 19, 198–
      200
    mutual fund market, 93–94
    stock market, 108–111,
      113, 115, 131–132
investment:
  as budget priority, 29–30,
    33–34, 37–38
  professional vs. amateurs, 90–
    91, 174–176, 179–180
  vs. speculation, 34–35

Investment Company Act of
  1940, 91

Johnson, Dr. Samuel, 111

Kennedy, Joseph P. (Ambassador), 59–60
Keogh plan, 91–92
Keynes, John Maynard, 193–
  194

land contracts, 84
Landfield, Sander, 112–113
lawyers, 175, 190
life insurance:
  annuities, 28–29, 36
  permanent, 26–28
  term, 25–27
  See also insurance

medical costs, 22–23, 30–31,
  53–54
medical insurance, 35–36, 39–
  40. *See also* insurance
money stocks, 123, 130–132,
  134–137. *See also* stocks
mortgages, 59–60, 74–75, 78,
  85
  advantages of, 61, 63, 67–70,
    74–75, 81–82
  long-term, 67–68, 70–71, 85
  payment and refinancing, 65–
    66, 72–73, 85–86
  variable, 71
  See also property
mutual funds:
  classifications, 88–89
  dividends, 99

general information on, 87, 91, 96, 101, 103–104, 174–175, 177–178, 181–184
  balanced, 93–94
  closed end, 98–99, 101–102
  growth, 93–94, 102
  load, 95
  no-load, 96–97, 100–101
  open end, 98, 101
  property, 64–65, 88, 146
investment in:
  conservative vs. speculative, 93, 138–139
  Keogh plan, 91–92
  long-term, 89–91, 99–100
  short-term, 89
management, 87–88, 92, 100–102
  charges (fees), 95–97
  sales malpractices, 104–105

natural resources stocks, 123–124, 132–134, 137–139, 141. *See also* stocks
New Deal, 15
New York Stock Exchange, 124, 185–186

Old Deal, 15

Penn Central Railroad, 52, 140–141, 154
price-earnings ratio, 110–111, 119–120
property:
  advantages as investment, 59–62, 65, 80–81, 83, 132, 175, 188–189
  construction, 78–79, 144–146
  forms of, 61
    agriculture, 83–84
    commercial/professional, 62
    income-producing, 70, 72–74
    property mutual funds, 64–65, 88, 146
    real estate investment trusts, 63–64
    sale/leaseback, 62
  vs. other type of investment, 70, 72, 77, 79–80, 82–83
  sale of, 66–67, 75–76, 84–85
  stocks, 144–146

recession, 17–18
rents, 23, 31–32, 59, 69–70
Rockefeller, John D., 32

savings. *See* cash reserve
savings accounts (deposits), 43–44, 47–48
savings certificates, 95
Securities Exchange Commission, 91, 184, 186–187
speculation, 34–35
  in bond market, 152
  in stock market, 39–40, 117–119, 137, 139, 143
stock certificates, 186–187, 189–190
stock market:
  effects of inflation on, 12–13, 19–20, 45
  effects of recession/depression/panic on, 17–18
  general information:
    distribution, 112–113
    new issues, 125–126
    over-the-counter market, 124–126

stock market (*cont.*)
  general information (*cont.*)
    price-earnings ratio, 110–111, 119–120
    price fluctuations, 106–111
    price indexes, 121–122, 124
    volume-price ratio, 108
    yield spread, 108–111, 113, 121–123
  historical information:
    bear market, 111–115
    bull market, 109–110
    the Depression, 14–16
    liquidity panic of 1907, 13–14
    stock market panic of 1917, 17
    today's problems, 11–12, 18–20, 106, 111–115, 173, 198–201
  See also stocks
stocks:
  categories, 121–124
    blue chip, 121–122, 126–127, 187
    "cats and dogs" (junk), 124
    conglomerates, 139
    cyclical, 122–123, 140–141
    growth (glamour), 121–122, 126–130
    money, 123, 130–132, 134–137
    natural resources, 123–124, 132–134, 137–139, 141
  "distressed," 116–117
  dividends, 99, 131
  "puts," 116
  sales malpractices, 104–105, 184–185

selection of, 146
specific information on:
  aerospace, 140–141, 182–183
  bank, 135–136
  Canadian, 144
  convertibles & preferred, 151, 166–167
  electronics, 118–119
  gold, 143
  health products, 142
  insurance, 134, 136
  natural gas, 138
  nursing homes, 141–142
  oil, 131–134
  pharmaceutical companies, 142–143
  property, 144–146
  uranium, 141
  utility, 130–132
  See also stock market

taxes:
  benefits (deductions):
    on mortgages, 63, 65, 67–69, 74–75
    on municipals, 168–169, 188
    on paid insurance policy, 39
    on property, 41, 63–64, 75–76, 132
  budgeting for, 30–31, 33
  increases in, 23, 31–32
  on investment income and gains:
    bonds, 150, 153–154, 161, 165
    mutual funds, 91–92, 99
    sale of property, 66–67, 84, 188–189

stocks, 117, 131–132, 189–190

time deposits, 43–44, 50–51

Treasury bills, 43–44, 49–51, 155–156, 164

Treasury bonds, 148, 155–158

Treasury notes, 156–157

trustee certificates, 154

U.S. Government:
"back-door" borrowing, 148–149
historical analysis of money problems, 12–16, 44–45

today's money crisis, 18–20, 106–108, 192–201

U.S. Treasury, 147–149, 155–157, 163–165, 168–169, 199. *See also* bonds; Treasury bills; Treasury notes; U.S. Government

volume-price ratio, 108

Warburg, Paul M., 13

yield-spread, 108–111, 118, 121–123